GROWTH & DEVELOPMENT OF
THE ENGLISH TOWN

AN ELIZABETHAN HOUSE AT RYE

This shows the enlarged window-space and the increasing use of brickwork.

Fr.   *Photo F. Frith and Co., Ltd.*

GROWTH & DEVELOPMENT OF
THE ENGLISH TOWN

BY

WRAY HUNT

AUTHOR OF
"GROWTH AND DEVELOPMENT OF THE
ENGLISH PARISH"

GEORGE G. HARRAP & COMPANY LTD.
LONDON   BOMBAY   SYDNEY

First published 1931
by GEORGE G. HARRAP & CO. LTD.
39-41 Parker Street, Kingsway, London, W.C.2

Printed in Great Britain by Jarrold & Sons, Limited, Norwich

TO

J. BERNARD BAKER, M.A. (Oxon.)

LATE CENSOR NON-COLLEGIATE
STUDENTS

PREFACE

IN every educational curriculum, from the elementary to the advanced, history has some place, usually an important place.

To meet the requirements of the different standards there is a bewildering supply of text-books, and it may seem proper to preface this book with something of an apology. The present work, however, is not a text-book; it is conceived on original lines, and is likely to justify itself as an attempt to stimulate that priceless possession of youth—imagination. If history is to be anything but an exercise of memory it should be so presented as to invite the reader to live in the period under consideration. Facts, dates, and names can never accomplish this; nay, rather they tend to repel, to stifle the imagination; that is, they become unreal. Similarly, broad outlines are too intangible; their vastness tends to appal.

Mr Wray Hunt has attempted to make great events understandable by picturing their effects on a small area. As no actual town could adequately present all the stages of development, all the reactions to leading events, he wisely asks us

The English Town

to imagine a town which can be taken as typical;
a composite conception which at any period will
remind the reader of any historical town that he
may happen to know. This book should stimulate
readers of all ages, and help to make what is too
often a dull subject deeply interesting.

J. BERNARD BAKER

CONTENTS

ILLUSTRATIONS

The English Town

GROWTH & DEVELOPMENT OF THE ENGLISH TOWN

CHAPTER I

The Beginning

IMAGINE a wild stretch of land, forest, and marsh and frowning hills; imagine a river, untamed, swift-flowing, making its way seaward, murmuring in still, deep stretches, brawling with hoarse grumbling over a stretch of shingle that forms a shallow, difficult to cross and dangerous, but when it is not in flood just possible for a strong and careful man, fairly easy for a horse.

Close to this ford is a tumbledown cluster of huts, wattle-and-daub affairs that remind one of the pictures in illustrated magazines of African villages. The forest is cleared for a space around this group of dwellings, probably by the primitive method of burning out, and a few patchy-looking fields of corn show yellow among the surrounding green. Lean, gaunt cattle graze among the marshes by the river, and if you enter the gloom of the oak woods you will come across herds of thin, fierce-looking swine that will in all probability run at a stranger, but answer the call of their herd, a bent, grizzled old fellow who dozes all day under a tree, for he has little to do except to take the herd out into the woods in the morning and bring them back at night. The very wolves know too much to attack a herd of these grim brutes, so unlike the fat and easygoing pig of the modern farmyard.

A very wild and primitive community dwell in these huts. Their clothes are rough, home-made stuff, a loose woollen garment like a long and clumsy shirt, skin shoes bound to the legs with thongs of the same material, and, if it is cold, a skin cloak worn with the hair inside. Yet, as the man who meets a cannibal chieftain clad in a smile and a top-hat, so the traveller in this age could guess that these people had come into touch with a higher civilization. He might find some of the wealthier men wearing, on high days and holidays, a ragged thing that had once been a toga, distinctive of the Roman citizen. Or he might discover a crude earthenware pot, bought from a wandering pedlar, upon whose brick-red surface was moulded the figure of a fat woman tied to a rock, while a clumsy-looking fellow stood over her with what was meant to be a sword, and at their feet crouched a distorted monster: the story of Perseus and Andromeda as depicted by the British craftsman in imitation of

PART OF A BRITISH VILLAGE AT CHRYSANTER, NEAR PENZANCE

Photo Gibson and Sons, Penzance

ROMAN BATH AT BATH

The basin and its surround are the original Roman masonry.
Courtesy L.M.S. Railway

The Beginning

his Roman master, not easy to recognize as such, because the Briton never could learn to paint of carve the human figure properly, probably because his Druid priests thought it for some reason wrong and irreligious to paint men except in a certain conventional pattern.

For in truth this wild village was not far from civilization. Within ten miles of it there ran, straight as an arrow, solid, purposeful, a great paved way, up and down which marched cohorts of soldiers, *tramp, tramp, tramp*, with the swing and beat of disciplined men with a fixed halting-place to be reached by a fixed hour. There were carriages too on that road, clumsy affairs, but quite serviceable. There were fortified cities along it, where sentinels in armour paced the watches up and down, up and down, while within the walls traders and pleasure-seekers pursued their aims. There were baths and luxury shops, and houses copied from those of great Rome, with central heating and colonnade and little groups of household gods, the latter probably kept secret, for officially the Empire was Christian. There would be churches too in these walled cities, where priests worshipped the new God who had come to upset all the old ideas of the Roman people. Ten miles from that lost wattle village all these things were to be found ; but ten miles is ten miles.

The English Town

Of course, if you have a motor-bus at your door, a good tarmac road, and a land where the motorist is the greatest danger you have to face upon your way, ten miles is a very little; one would travel as far as that for a day's fishing; much farther for many sorts of business and pleasure. But ten miles through a thick forest, by a path that for six months of the year is much more like a rather dirty stream-bottom, and even in summer can plunge the unwary walker up to his thighs in slush, is a different matter. Ten miles need some courage to tackle when the path wanders through a forest where wolves are quite common, and where dwells that most dangerous of all wild beasts, the boar, who, as the writer knows by experience in other lands, does not wait for provocation to charge. Ten miles may mean a night in such a forest, and that would be a terrifying experience for people who, apart from the real dangers of the place, believed in every form of malicious spirit and goblin that the mind of man has ever imagined.

So this village remained, primitive, wild, self-contained, self-satisfied, but ten miles away from civilization. True, the two worlds—the world of the forest and the world of the Roman road—sometimes met for a short while, and sometimes a man would leave the one for the other, when some uncouth forest villager, for reasons of his own, went off and joined a legion of Roman soldiers. But he never came back, for the Romans never employed locally enlisted men near their own homes. Probably he went up north to the Wall, or south to Portus Ithicus, and died by a Pictish arrow or a Saxon battleaxe. Possibly he might end his days in far-away Gaul, where rival emperors fought for the throne of the Empire that in the end the barbarians, the bearded men from the outer borders of the Empire, seized for themselves.

At other times a Roman magistrate—that is, a Briton born, but a Roman citizen, and employed by the Empire, just as a village Tahsildar in India to-day, though Indian born, is a servant of the English king—would hold court, and listen to such problems as the forest village could not itself solve by its own constitution. But these occasions were few and far between, and the work of experts has proved that the great civilized Roman town and the half-savage British village existed at the same time, for the remains of both have been dug up and examined, and those whose business it is to study these things say that both were of about the same date.

Now to answer a question that I am sure every reader is asking in his own mind: Why not begin

the story of an English town with the story of
one of these civilized towns instead of a mere
village in the forest? The reason is that only a
few of these proud Roman towns remain to-day
as towns. Some are mere villages, some lost altogether, some buried beneath the outer suburbs of
modern towns. For some reason the new owners
of the land, of whose coming this story has now
to tell, did not like to build their homes on the
site of Roman towns and villages, and only the
greatest of the Roman cities, such as York and
London and Chester, have survived to become
English towns. But as this book treats of the
commonplace town of England, not the great
cities, it is better to show how most of these
commonplace towns grew up.

For the settled state of affairs that I have
shown did not last for ever. There came a day
when the feet of marching soldiers no longer
echoed on the paving of that straight road, when
the walled cities lay silent and trembling, for no
longer did the challenge of the sentry, the sharp
answer of the officer of the guard going his rounds,
tell them that all was well. Sentry and officer
were gone, marching away southward toward the
Channel ports, on their way to Gaul or to Rome,
where the very heart of the Empire was exposed
to the ferocity of the barbarian.

The Beginning

The Wall was no longer the Wall men had known; lonely, ungarrisoned, it stood, a mockery of its old, strong self. Imagine if you can the feelings of a man of to-day if he woke up to hear that the Navy was no more, that the ships that hold the seas lay rusting at their anchors, so that any man who would might destroy our shipping and invade our shores.

Yet to-day we are at peace. There are no fierce pirates swarming off our coasts, and though it is a comic-paper joke that the Scots have never ceased invading England, their coming does not now mean a ghastly glare in the sky where the towns along their road go up in flames, or a huddle of tortured corpses fouling the air behind them. But in the days of which I write the coming of the Scots did mean this; the Wall was undefended and there was nothing more to stop them.

The Count of the Saxon Shore was gone too, the great officer who had held with his swift-moving, ruthless cohorts the eastern coasts of our lands, punishing the fierce, yellow-haired pirates who even then swept in their long ships out of the cold sea and left behind them the silence of death. Maybe the last of the Counts of the Saxon Shore is still remembered. It is just possible that one man, half-Briton, half-Roman, stuck to his post and fought while life remained to him in defence

The English Town

of his trust, and that that one man was the original Arthur about whose name legends have clustered as bees about the honeysuckle.

At first these stirring events affected our village not at all. Now and then a breath from the outer world whispered among the leaves of their forest some tale of blood and desolation that would cause shivering panic to-day among people living a hundred miles from the scene of the tragedy. But in the youth of our country villages and tribes were self-contained, self-satisfied. It mattered little to one group that another group very far away had been slaughtered and their homes burnt—that was bad luck for the sufferers; but, after all, who had ever even heard the name of their home till it was brought on the wings of rumour? And in any case life was hard enough without bothering about the troubles of distant, unknown folk. So the village in the forest continued its daily life, with its little tragedies and its little comedies, as it had since long before the Romans came to the land.

Then one day something happened that woke the village in the forest to sudden hopeless panic. There was no warning, no foreknowledge of disaster. One night the villagers went to sleep as they had always done, careless of the morrow, tired by the work of the day, this man dreaming

The Beginning

that he would go into the forest and gather fuel for the stack that stood beside his house; this that he would take a day with bow and arrow and see if a little meat could not be procured for a festival soon to take place—a wedding perhaps; this counting over the rich store of corn that would fill the village bins. . . .

Then came the ship, sailing from the terrible unknown expanse of the sea, up the wide mouth of the river that ran past the village. Wondering, the villagers gathered upon the shore to watch this new thing disturbing the ancient order of their life.

None of them had ever seen such a ship. It was long, very unlike the tubby wicker affairs in which they sometimes ventured to the river-mouth seeking a few fish to add to their diet, or to sell to a travelling pedlar, who would buy from them for the supply of some distant feast inland, where a Roman with the luxurious tastes of his race was willing to pay good prices for a feast of fish. It had a high mast, with a great square sail, and looked as terrible as it was. The high prow was carved into the shape of a serpent's head, the stern resembled the tail of some monstrous dragon of the waters, and the decks were crowded with men.

Tall, light-haired, with fierce, seamed faces and long, drooping moustaches, they were; and each

The English Town

man carried a sword and spear, and had a bull's-hide shield slung upon his left arm. The villagers looked at each other, amazed and horror-stricken. These were the terrible men from the sea of whom they had heard such tales. Hastily the elders caught up such arms as they possessed, feeble bows that shot clumsy bronze-tipped arrows a few yards, well enough against the wild beasts of the forest that had no shields and could not throw back weapons, though even against them they failed often enough, but poor weapons indeed to use against these well-armed warriors. Their other weapons were similar, weak, puny tools, very unsuited to serious combat.

For these people of the forest had forgotten how to fight. They had lived under the Roman peace, when private war between man and man or tribe and tribe had been put down with a stern hand. They were not like their brethren of the West, who had escaped the Roman yoke and were still fighters born and bred. Very little hope had they of defeating these terrible men, the more so as the ship's crew outnumbered the inhabitants of the village.

But they were not going to give in without a fight. They stood bravely to their arms and waited, ranked together on the shore, hoping against hope to beat off the invaders.

The Beginning

Vain hope! Steadily the strange ship turns her nose shoreward, the men at the oars bend to their work, and, like the serpent she represents, the ship glides through the water till her sharp prow grates on the bank. Then, as one man, the rowers spring from their thwarts, and, seizing sword and spear, fling themselves upon the wretched folk on shore.

From the first the fight was hopeless. The Britons had never been trained to fight. There was among them one retired legionary, a man who had drilled and fought under Roman officers in the Roman style, but one man could not put heart into a crowd that fought as a crowd, not as an army, every man for himself, his home, and his little ones. Brave enough they were, but they lacked the discipline and unity that go to make successful soldiers, and the fierce, warlike men from the sea broke through their ranks as the flood bursts an insufficient dam.

Howling, the wretched villagers fled to the forest, but even there was no safety for them; their pursuers followed, sparing neither man, woman, nor child while the fury of battle lasted. At last, when night fell, there were left of the villagers in the forest but a few cowering fugitives, who must either starve in the woods where they lay hidden, or work their way westward, a dangerous, possibly a useless, journey, till they reached some town or village unconquered by the heathen from over the sea, or else be made slaves by the new conquerors.

That this happened to many there can be no doubt. Words in modern language—'bacon,' for instance—have been traced back to British sources, and most of these words are similar, domestic terms that a slave might well use and his master copy from him.

Left in possession of the village, the conquerors proceeded in their usual fashion. The pitiful cluster of huts was burned to the ground, the site deserted. For these Angles were superstitious folk—they feared the ghosts of their dead enemies if they should build where those had lived. But at another point a little higher up the river, where the ford was, they set to work to raise a village, enclosed, for there was always danger of attack, by a stout wood pallisade. With blows and curses the poor survivors of the conquered were driven to build this new fortress.

Ellington they called it, for the name of the fierce-eyed leader was Ella, and his tribe, the Ellings, gave their own name to the town they built. There they settled, and began to clear the forest for cultivation, living meanwhile on the products of the chase and the cattle and swine captured from the unfortunate Britons.

The Beginning

That, or something like it, is the first stage in the growth of many an English town; and I have tried to picture the hurried catastrophe that overwhelmed the Britons tribe by tribe, village by village, till, one hundred years after the first coming of the pirates, Britain became Angle-land, and the Romans were as if they had never been, except for a few traces here and there of their long occupation. The stage was set for the next act.

CHAPTER II
The Village

THESE conquerors, though they had come as pirates, did not mean to continue that uncertain life. They had been driven from their own homes along the bleak German shore by hunger and by the influx of other and stronger tribes from the East, and sought overseas a new home where they could live as they had lived in their old German land. Indeed, it is noticeable that not very long after these people landed in Britain they had lost their old skill at sea, and Alfred the Great had to offer the rank of thegn, or small noble, to any merchant who would fare overseas three times at his own costs, and to hire Frisians from the Dutch coast to man his ships that he built against the Danes.

So the new folk, the Ellings, set to work to divide up their newly won land. The wide, cleared area was split up into two great fields, huge, rough areas of arable land. One of these was to be ploughed up in one year, while the other rested, and *vice versa*. This was because there was no system of manuring the land or

26

changing the crops, by which means we avoid to-day the waste that resulted from this primitive system.

Then the fields themselves were divided out among the villagers. But nobody actually owned land; the tribe as a whole was the only land-owner. The reason for this is plain enough. If a man owns land that man must supply fences, barns, ploughs, beasts to work the ploughs, all before he can begin to make a profit out of his farm. But for that a man needs capital, either in the form of money or of spare time during which he can work at these things, without neglecting the work by which he gets his actual living. These people had neither of these things. Money hardly existed among these wild conquerors of our land, and as for spare time, while a man was making barns and ploughs and hedges he would starve. The only thing was for all to club together. Then some could get the essential sowing and reaping done, while others made hedges, barns, and other necessaries. Thus the work could go forward, and the man who had done less than his share in the fields, but had shown skill as a carpenter, was paid by being given a share of the crops as big as the rest who had done his part of the field-work.

The arrangement was that each man was allotted so many long, narrow strips of ground scattered round the field, to the produce of which he was entitled. The number of strips varied; for instance, in the town of our story Ella, as chief, would be given the largest number of strips. The greater warriors of the tribe would be given the next greatest number, then the common warriors would receive their share; last of all the serfs, either of their own or the conquered race, received their little patches. Then the work of the village would be divided out, this man doing the plough-ing, while that man acted as village herd, or bee-keeper, or repaired the implements of the farm when they were damaged. The produce of the farm would at harvest be divided out: so much for a man with twenty strips, half that amount for one with ten. But the poorer landholders probably got more than their exact share as payment for their work in the village outside the fields.

Beside the fields were the great expanses of common pasture and waste. The pasture was more or less cleared, fit for grazing cattle and sheep, and each villager might keep a certain number of beasts on the pasture, according to the number of strips that he held in the common field. The waste was virgin woodland, where the commoners might gather fuel and feed their swine, though probably from the earliest times the right

The Village

to hunt the beasts of the chase was reserved to the richer and greater men of the village; and when in course of time the king became ruler over all these scattered settlements he took these rights and granted them with sparing hand to his followers.

Here, then, in Ellington was such a little self-contained community, the germ of the future town as the acorn is the germ of the future oak. The township, as this sort of village was called, needed but two things from the outer world, salt and iron, and these, when required in greater quantities than could be secured locally, were carried round by pedlars with trains of horses. All the rest they made themselves.

As we have seen, the folk of this town of ours grew their own food, milked their own cows, killed such meat as they ate, which was not much. They sheared their own sheep too, and the women of the village worked the wool up into cloth, and made the garments needed by their families. Soft leather shoes were also made at home. The plough was an affair of the most primitive sort. A large forked branch of a tree served as the body of the instrument. To the longer branch of the fork were fitted rings or pegs to hold the harness for the four great oxen who dragged the plough. The short end of the fork was sharpened, shod with

29

iron, and used to scratch rather than plough the ground. The clumsy sickles for reaping were made by the village smith, an important person, whose trade title is now the commonest surname in England. There was no need for any denizen of Ellington to travel away from his birthplace, and for many years it was a rare thing for any of them to do so. Wheelwright, wainwright, smith, these were the crafts required by the simple village of the English, and probably in early days all three were combined in the one man.

But changes did take place, slow changes, unnoticed by the people who lived while they were taking place except when some sudden outbreak of battle, murder, and sudden death, brought about by the changes as they took place, woke the village of Ellington from its peaceful ways. First the group of tribes to which the Ellings belonged sailed over one by one from their old home and settled in the district, ousting or enslaving the old inhabitants, and when this process was complete the country was comparatively well populated. There were huge tracts of waste land, but when methods were so primitive as in these early days they were needed. It would take four or five times the area of land to keep a man supplied with food that would be needed for that purpose to-day. The result was that disputes and struggles broke out between neighbouring villages over questions such as boundary and pasture. Ella's son Wulfstan, for instance, fought a pitched battle with a neighbouring thegn, Brithnoth of Halsham, over a grazing squabble. Brithnoth, defeated, applied to a neighbour for aid, and Wulfstan did the same. Soon the whole district was ablaze with warfare, and there was a good deal of burning of villages and raiding of cattle. Finally the trouble settled down when a chieftain, Offa by name, the leader of the largest tribe in the area, defeated Wulfstan's party and promptly set himself up as overlord of the whole district, ordering both sides in the quarrel to submit to his decision.

That was the beginning of the kingship. Hitherto the title 'king' appears to have meant the head priest or wisest man of any area, but now the word begins to take its modern meaning. Offa thus became king of the people of this group of tribes, and soon the whole district became known as the Sword-folk's land, and Offa as king of the Sword-folk.

No longer was Ellington a mere isolated unit, owing obedience to no man. It was a definite part of a kingdom, a hundred, as this division, a village and its surrounding land, came to be called. No longer was the folk-moot, the gathering of the tribe beneath some sacred tree, the sole authority that could make the laws and dispense justice. It still continued to exist, as the hundred moot, but there was another and larger court, that of King Offa himself, at which the thegn or chief of Ellington must attend, and at which would be heard cases between an inhabitant of Ellington and of some other village. No longer is the thegn of Ellington sole ruler of his own village. He is but one of many thegns, subject to a king. It is the first beginning of a State. As it had begun the process continued. Soon the Sword-folk themselves lost their separate existence, the greater kingdom of Mercia under savage old Penda swallowed them up; the Sword-folk's land became a shire, a share of the greater kingdom. The hundred court continued, so did the king's court of the Sword-folk, but now it was called the shire court, and in place of a king an ealdorman presided over it, owing allegiance to the distant Penda.

With the quarrels that followed we are not concerned. Wessex, Mercia, and Northumbria fought for power in England, till at length, under the sickly Alfred, a mighty spirit in a feeble frame, Wessex won the victory. Had Alfred been other than he was that might have been but a prelude to further warfare, but Alfred was an English king and tried to make England a nation. He failed, but showed the way to others.

Meanwhile, while kingdoms rose and fell,

The Village

something else happened in quiet, out-of-the-way Ellington. First, as the mist heralds the dawning, came confused stories of a new God, very like Balder the Beautiful, the sun-god of the Angles, the only one of all their gods who was not a fierce, brutal warrior lusting for slaughter. This God, it was said, had died and come to life again, just as Balder did when shot by blind Hoder at Loki's instigation with the mistletoe arrow that alone could harm him. He was gentle and kindly, and men called Him the " White Christ."

Then one day there came from the South a stranger. That in itself was an event that brought the whole village flocking to see a new thing. But this stranger was quite unlike anybody that any of the folk had ever seen before. For one thing, he was close shaven, and most of the folk of Ellington wore beards, or at least large moustaches. Then his dress was peculiar, a long, black robe gathered at the waist by a cord. He carried neither sword nor spear, and that was unusual for a traveller in those dangerous days. Instead, he carried high before his face a great image, two pieces of wood crossed, and upon them the figure of a Man.

This, the folk of Ellington decided, must be magic, especially as the stranger seemed to speak to it in a strange tongue as he walked. But the

c

stranger paused in his going and asked, in gentle tones, for food.

The people of Ellington were not inhospitable, but they were somewhat frightened. It was some time before any man would move, and then only at the direct order of Elfric the Thegn, whose bull voice roared at some of his men to hasten and bring food to the wanderer. The truth was that Elfric was curious about this wonderful visitor from the dimness of the outer world, and, while half frightened of witchcraft, anxious to know more about him. So, when the man was fed, Elfric advanced toward him.

" Who are you, stranger," he asked, " and what is that thing you carry with you? "

At that the stranger began to speak, setting his image upright in the ground before him. The villagers gathered round fascinated. This man was preaching of the White Christ, of Whom they had heard rumours. The story, so familiar to us, was fresh to them, and, childlike, these early ancestors of ours loved a story. So they listened with interest to the old monk's tale. It was certainly a very wonderful story, of One Who was born a Son of God, Who died far away in the East, in a wonderful land of which they had never heard before, and Who rose again after three days.

" He speaks of Balder," muttered one to

A SHIP OF ALFRED'S NAVY
Gilbert James

34

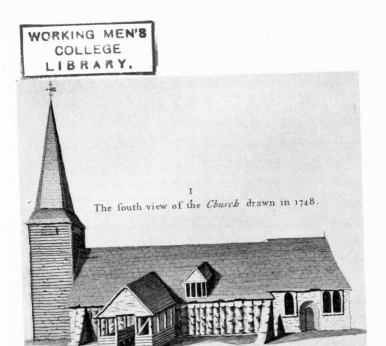

I
The south view of the *Church* drawn in 1748.

ANGLO-SAXON WOODEN CHURCH AT GREENSTEAD, NEAR ONGAR

The nave of this little church is one of the most ancient buildings in England, dating back to at least 1013. It is said that the bones of St Edmund rested within its timbered walls in 1013, when on their way from London for final interment at St Edmund's Bury. These walls were built of the trunks of trees hewn more than nine hundred years ago, some of which still stand in their original position; outside they were untrimmed, but inside the nave the marks of the axe are to be seen upon them.

From a print in the British Museum.

35

another, as the tale went on. " It is Balder the Beautiful."

But it was not. Gradually the folk began to understand what this man was demanding: that they should give up their old gods and believe in one God only, and in this White Christ, His Son, Who was, in some un-understandable way, one with the Father. It was at first a matter for surprised angry protest. Ulf, the priest of Odin, objected violently to the blasphemy, and the loss of profits that would occur if this stranger had his way. But the thegn was disposed to listen. He was a man of some intelligence, and this new faith appeared to him far less improbable and confused than the jumble of tales that was the religion of his folk. Also, he had heard that the King of Wessex had accepted this new faith, and indeed it was said that his own Mercian lord, now that Penda was dead, was considering it. Thirdly, this man seemed wise and learned ; he might be persuaded to stay with them and teach them some of his secrets if they accepted his faith.

So the monk stayed and preached, and soon, from laughing at him, men began to listen and one by one adopted his new teaching.

" It is Ragnarok, the Twilight of the Gods," cried the priest of Odin, as one by one his flock left him to follow the White Christ. " The end of all things is near."

Soon the whole village was Christian. For it seems from what records we have that these old ancestors of the English were tolerant folk. They did not burn and kill the priests of the new faith. Sometimes they accepted their teaching, sometimes laughed at them, sometimes drove them out of the country, but rarely killed. Wessex, Northumbria, Mercia, accepted the new teaching, Sussex alone remaining pagan till turbulent Wilfred of York, driven out of his own church, became its missionary.

So there rose in Ellington a little wooden church, close to the old Odin stone, where a priest baptized and wedded the folk and preached the new faith. But still the life of the people was little disturbed. They were wise men, these early Christian missionaries to England, and disturbed the habits of their converts as little as possible. When they found that certain days were set apart for feasting in honour of the gods they merely substituted a Christian for a heathen feast. Thus the great mid-winter feast of Yule became Christmas, and the midsummer feast that of St John. May Day took on a new religious guise. Even the old gods did not vanish. Weland, the smith of the gods, became Weyland Smith who shoes horses for travellers. Odin and Thor became giants and ogres, and to this day popular legends such as Jack the Giant-killer keep them in memory.

But the new religion really made great changes, though so slowly that men failed to recognize them. In the first place, this faith was under one head. The Pope at Rome gave his orders, and those orders penetrated down to the poorest parish priest in the most remote of parishes. There was at last in England one force that was strong and united, that set its face against the constant private feuds of the tribes, and helped to unite England.

But peace led, as always, to plenty. It was worth while now for the people of Ellington, as of the rest of England, to try to improve their methods a little, and to have a little over each year, for they need not fear as much as before lest some rival tribe should destroy all their work. Then, too, a number of monks settled down in a building that they put up for themselves, quarrying the stone from the old Roman road, and began to till the land. But these men could read and write, accomplishments regarded as magical or near it by the wild folk of Ellington, and from their books they could discover better methods of farming.

Feebly the folk of Ellington began to copy the

monks' ideas. They stuck to their old common
field system, for the monks themselves knew no
better, but they did try to improve the breed of
cattle and sheep a little, and to farm more cleanly.
Thus they had a little surplus, which the monks
would sometimes buy, for they needed plenty of
food to feed their huge establishment, and the
poor for whom they cared, and the little group of
scholars whom they taught, and if they bought
they paid in money, hitherto practically unknown
to the folk of Ellington.

So through the years the people of Ellington
grew a little better off, more civilized, less fierce,
and softer, till a new and terrible danger forced
them to fight for their very lives, and changed
the course of their history.

CHAPTER III

The Danelagh

REALLY the turning-point of Ellington's history comes when the Danes descended upon the English coast. It was these terrible pirates who changed the stagnant village into a slowly growing town, though at first it seemed that they would do to Ellington what fierce old Ella, whose very name his descendants had now forgotten, had done to that little British village in the forest.

For, just as Ella's long ship had sailed up the river and attacked the forest village, so one dim, windy morning another yet more terrible-looking vessel worked its way up the stream toward Ellington. It was the warship of a Norse chieftain, Eric of the Bloody Axe, who lived upon the shores of a deep fiord in distant Norway. He was a Viking, a fierce, independent, sea-rover, living head of his own little tribe in his *Vik* or bay—for the name ' Viking ' does not mean ' sea-king ' as is sometimes asserted—and for ever fighting against the attempts of the king who dwelt down in the southern quarter of Norway to secure control of his kingdom.

It was very well for Ellington that there was

The English Town

a monastery close at hand, for these early Viking raiders were not, like the early English, looking for new homes. Their object was a shipful of plunder, gold for preference, and that was more easily got from a rich monastery than a poor village. For already during the hundred years or so that Ellington and its district had been Christian, men had given great gifts to the monks for their souls' sake, and there were jewelled cups and golden crosses and other treasures within the walls of the monastery. So Eric contented himself with burning down the wood-and-daub village of Ellington and killing any of its inhabitants who were not quick enough in getting away to the forest; he did not wait to complete the massacre, but hurried on to the monastery, where he secured a valuable cargo to take home with him to distant Norway.

That was the beginning of a terrible time for the folk of Ellington. Three times in the next forty years their homes were burned about their heads, three times the wretched folk had to flee to the forest, where not a few died of starvation and cold. But always there were a few left who, because they knew nowhere else to go, crept miserably back to their ruined homes when the raiders had gone and set to work to repair the terrible destruction wrought by the Norsemen.

VIKING SHIPS

THE TOWN OF DUNSTER

A typical English town, surrounded by woods and meadows, and clustering about the old parish church. The eleventh-century castle suggests feudal overlordship.

Photo J. Dixon-Scott

The Danelagh

" From the fury of the Norsemen, good Lord deliver us! "

The petition arose from every church in England during those dark days, but only one man in all the land was willing to add deeds to prayers, only one man could realize that God helps those who help themselves; and that man was Alfred of Wessex, who fought the invaders on their own chosen element, the sea, and in the end kept his country English.

But Ellington was in Mercia, close to the East Anglian border, and for that land there was no peace, for its people would not combine against the enemy. Each village and shire must do what it could for itself, for the royal family of Mercia were too busy quarrelling among themselves to organize their subjects against the Danes. So, when Alfred, after defeating Guthrun at Chippenham, made a treaty with him, Ellington became part of the Danelagh, that portion of England that came under Danish rule. Instead of their English ealdorman the folk of Ellington came under the rule of a Danish jarl, and in place of the easygoing Ethelbald, descendant of Ella, a Danish thegn came to dwell at the wooden hall that dominated the little clustered houses of the village. The English inhabitants retained their holdings of land, but on stricter terms. Now they

The English Town

must work so many days a week upon the land of Edric, the new ruler of the village, and were less free in many little ways than they had been before.

Yet this disaster proved the beginning of new things for the village of Ellington, as for many another English village and town. For the Danes, as the English called Dane and Norseman alike, were not only pirates: they were skilled traders as well, fearless travellers, unlike the stay-at-home English, and had an eye for the most suitable points for trading-centres. Derby, Nottingham, and Leicester owe their greatness to the Danes, who turned little English townlets into great trading-towns.

So it was with Ellington. There was a river up which ships could come from the wide seas so many miles away, and a little above the village was a ford where the river could be crossed. Edric saw the advantages of such a site, and soon in a small way trade began to grow about the village of Ellington.

For Edric built a wooden wharf down below the ford, and sent his own ship coasting down as far as London, or even over the narrow seas to France to buy cloth and spices, sending out cargoes of corn, hides, or wool to sell again, and when the ship came home, salt-crusted and battered, and tied up to the crazy wooden pier, then her cargo was unloaded by sweating Englishmen. Edric paid for this labour, and his pay was accepted gladly by holders of poor strips in the common fields. The goods were stored in a great warehouse down by the wharf.

Then, when the roads were dry and the weather favourable, Edric would load up his goods on pack-ponies and trudge away to Leicester or Derby, there to sell the goods at a fine thumping profit in the busy markets of those towns.

Edric the Thegn was not the only person to profit by this trading. In their own way the villagers of Ellington shared the prosperity, for there were extra tasks always needing hands to do them, and a man could earn quite a few pennies in a year—and a penny was wealth to the poor English villager of those days—by doing extra tasks for the trading thegn, accompanying him on his journeys, or even sailing in his ship, though for this few of the English villagers had either the skill or the courage.

Besides, Edric was not the only trader in the land. There were others who moved slowly, and amid great perils and hardships, up and down the tracks which served for roads. Again, the village of Ellington won profit from the movements of trade, for the bridge that had once spanned the river ten miles higher up had long since vanished like its builders. There was no crossing-place between Ellington and the sea, so that he who wished to travel from East Anglia up into Eastern Mercia or Northumbria must cross the river at Ellington or go some twelve miles farther inland to the next practicable ford. So when the roads were dry there was quite a number of pedlars and chapmen passing through the one narrow, straggling street that made up the village of Ellington, and there was money to be gained by selling eggs and milk and bread to these travellers. Edwin of the Ford, a man whose little hut lay some small way above the village near the ford, began to grow quite wealthy, for he knew the safe and the dangerous parts of the crossing, and for one little farthing would wade through the swirling water, leading the traveller's horse.

Soon Edwin was adding to his income in another way. For the ford was not always passable. After a summer storm the traveller must spend a night on the bank, waiting for the water to go down. For men of rank the thegn's hall was open. Edric would receive and entertain his equals, nor charge a penny. For poorer folk there was the monastery. But the monastery was some way off; a man in a hurry would prefer to be close to his road, ready to take advantage of the first fall in the level of the river.

So the cunning Edwin built a shed outside his

The Danelagh

hut, where for a farthing the traveller and his beasts might have shelter, and his wife, Edith, would supply, for a little extra money, a good meal to cheer the traveller on his way. When he died Edwin left his son well on the way to becoming one of the innkeepers, such as Chaucer's Harry Bailey of the " Tabard," famous in *The Canterbury Tales*, who provided for the needs of the English roads.

Then there were the pilgrims. That was after Edric's death, when once again the Danes came to England and put to death an English archbishop and many another Englishman—aye, and Christian Dane. Among them was Christopher, abbot of the monastery of St Jude, near Ellington, burned alive in his own abbey by a host of furious Vikings from whose greedy, sacrilegious clutch he had saved the Abbey treasures, hiding them where the closest search failed to bring them to light. Then, after the storm, came an interval of calm, when Canute, a Christian—at any rate, while in England, though some of the stories of his behaviour when he went back to his own land are not exactly Christian—reigned over Wessex and the Danelagh alike. Soon strange tales began to spread about the Abbot Christopher. Men said that the sick had been cured, the blind received their sight, the lame walked, when they touched the holy tomb of the martyr, and from all over East Anglia and Mercia pilgrims began to flock to Ellington to seek the relief from their ills offered by the tomb of this good man.

The monastery hospice received all that it could. But there were those that must lie without the monastery, and Gurth the Lame, who could earn little money because of his crippled state, began to accommodate travellers. There was young Alfred too, a clever boy well trained in wood-carving by the good monks of St Jude's monastery, who found that there was profit to be made by his skill. For grateful pilgrims would pay, and pay well, for little wooden replicas of the good abbot's shrine to take home with them and keep in memory of their pilgrimage, and Alfred began to grow rich.

So little by little the town began to grow and the population to increase. This was the natural result of prosperity. In a poor village children died like flies when times were bad, but Ellington brought to manhood more children than the average village, for its mothers were better nourished and its little ones better cared for. Of course, to our ideas the deaths among the children reached appalling figures; a man who had ten children and saw four grow to twenty years of age was fortunate, but the poorer villages in the neighbourhood were even worse off. People from distant parts too would now and then wander into Ellington and settle there. One or two cross-streets began to spring up off the main village street.

The people of Ellington disliked these 'foreigners,' as they called any not born in their own village, but Sweyn, the far-seeing lord of the village encouraged them. They had to pay him toll for permission to settle down, and he also got a certain petty tax on every deal between an inhabitant of Ellington and an outsider, so it paid him to foster the trade of the little town. He also got dues on every ship that put in to the harbour that his grandfather Edric had built on the river-bank, and nowadays quite a number of ships began to use that harbour, for continual coming and going had tramped out quite a good road from Ellington to Leicester, and the harbour, though a ship must sail a long way up the river to get to it, had two advantages. First, it was nearer the centres of trade than many a bigger port close to the sea, an important point when land travel was expensive and more dangerous even than water travel; secondly, there was a shallow bank of mud just opposite the quay, where a ship might be drawn up for cleansing, and no danger, as near the open sea, of some sudden storm battering the timbers of the vessel's bottom to pieces as she lay careened on her side to be scraped.

The English Town

But it must not be imagined that Ellington was yet anything that we should call a town. The main body of the folk were still mere farmers; even the tradesmen managed their portion of the common field, trading in their spare time, between seed-time and harvest, or taking a day off their field-work now and then to work on the wharf. If a man journeyed to Nottingham or Leicester or Derby he left his son to look after his share of the field in his place. It was but a large village, with a small trading community added to its population of farmers and herdsmen.

Soon the people of Ellington began to find that prosperity has its dangers and its disadvantages. Trade attracts rogues as sugar attracts flies, and is, moreover, capricious and uncertain. This year will be good, next year bad. A rich man to-day may have bad luck and become a poor man to-morrow. Take the case of Sigbert, skilful with his needle, who bought a bale of cloth in Nottingham, meaning to make some money by repairing or remaking garments for pilgrims and travellers, who often arrived after a hard journey almost in rags. Passing through the forest on his way back to Ellington, Sigbert was robbed and stripped, arriving at his home at last in a few miserable rags given him by a charitable charcoal-burner, having begged his way from hall to hall and monastery to monastery. The poor man was ruined, and must start all over again from nothing. Then there was Rolf the shipman, drowned at sea, leaving a widow and five children in dire poverty, who must have starved but that their neighbours cared for them, and that Sweyn, in whose service the father had perished, gave the children holdings from his own demesne, the land that he had reserved for himself, as the overlords of villages were now beginning to do, keeping apart some portion of the land from the common stock of the village.

So the idea began to grow up of what afterward became the gild. The better-off villagers banded themselves together for mutual protection and took the name of the patron saint of the monastery for that of their brotherhood. It was a simple association, to which any man who would or could pay a penny a year and half a pound of wax could belong, and women too were admitted. Every year, upon the feast-day of St Jude, there was a meeting of the brotherhood at the parish church, where the priest preached a special sermon for their benefit, having first said a solemn Mass for the brethren and sisters of the gild.

But the main business of the association was to care for the sick and aged who had fallen upon evil days, instead of leaving them to the chance

D

The English Town

charity of the lord or their neighbours. Any brother or sister who had paid his penny was entitled to be helped from the gild stock in case of need. Gradually, too, the custom grew up that a brother or sister who by good luck or skill got a little more money than his or her companions should give a little of it to the gild stock, or leave something to the aldermen and brethren when he or she died, for the benefit of the gild.

It was a very primitive association, this early gild; indeed it is doubtful if it was called a ' gild ' at all, but there is evidence of some such organization in many English towns even before the Norman Conquest, so we may well suppose that the rising, thriving townlet of Ellington would not be among the last to develop an institution of the kind. Certain it is that among the earliest documents to be found dealing with our towns are copies of the rules of such gilds as that here described, and they were of immense importance in the life of the town that was to be.

For the moment, however, the peaceful growth of Ellington received a rude and sudden check when William the Norman, having been promised the throne of England by his imbecile cousin, Edward the Confessor, descended on England's shores to claim what he declared to be his rights. He was followed by an army composed of half the riff-raff of feudal Europe, Normans, Frenchmen, Flemings, Bretons, Italians, Germans, gathered under the banner of one in whose veins mingled the blood of fierce Norseman and polished Frenchman. It is a misnomer to talk of the Norman Conquest; the conquest was the work of William of Normandy, but it is doubtful if even half his army were of Norman birth or descent.

Ellington took no part in the resistance of Harold Godwinson to the Conqueror, for it was in Mercia, and the stupidly selfish Morcar, Earl of Mercia, refused to help his old enemy Harold, hoping to make good terms with the Conqueror if Harold were, as Morcar secretly hoped, defeated. But he had misjudged his man. William of Normandy had no use for traitors, and Morcar lost his earldom and his life.

In the next chapter will be described the fate of Ellington under the new harsh rule that made England the great country that we know. Like the rest of England, Ellington had to pass through the fire, to learn, in the school of adversity, discipline and self-control and patriotism, and, like the rest of England, Ellington did not like the process of learning. But it had to be, and on the whole the towns of England gained much from the coming of iron-handed, iron-hearted William and his motley crew of followers.

CHAPTER IV

Under the Norman

AT first the conquest of England by the Normans made little difference to the people of Ellington. After all, within the preceding two hundred years England had twice been conquered by Danish invaders, yet the life of the country had continued along more or less the same lines. There was nothing to warn the ordinary Englishman that this new conquest was to prove different.

But he was soon to learn. For William the Norman was no common raider. He had conquered England, and he meant to rule it. Himself the most turbulent of the vassals of the King of France, he did not intend to allow others to treat him as he treated his overlord. The strict Continental feudal system took the place of the loose English system. The king owned all the land, and those who held portions held them on strict terms. If of gentle rank—freemen, in fact—they must do military service, so many armed knights for forty days in each year, in return for so much land. Those who tilled the land were known as villeins and must do a strictly enforced amount of task work on their lord's land. The half-free English churl became the unfree villein. On the other hand, actual slavery ceased to exist. The villein was bound to the soil, not to its lord. He might not leave his manor, as the village with its waste and forest came to be called, but the lord of the manor had not complete power over his villein, as the slave-owner had over his slave.

This was especially the case in England, for in order to make the great landowners less dangerous William allowed the shire courts to continue, and handed over to them the consideration of more serious cases. The old hundred court had for some time been almost a private court, and now in most cases the lord's manor court took its place, but it could not deal with serious crime, that must be sent to the sheriff, a royal officer who had for long taken the place of the ealdorman as president of the shire court.

The law, too, was strictly enforced. The good old easy days when a landholder who owed the king service for his land did it or not as his fancy dictated were over for good. William expected his pound of flesh, and a little over for good weight when he could get it, which was disliked enough by his own followers, but far more by the English, particularly such of them as had been allowed to retain their lands, for they had not learned the meaning of discipline. Also, the patriotism of those who had deserted Harold in his peril began to awake now that they saw the full results of their stupidity. So when Hereward roused the fen country Sibald of Ellington, son of Sweyn, marched off with as many as would join him to the Camp of Refuge at Ely.

He never came back. Vague rumours flew back to Ellington, tales of witchcraft and disaster, but of the twenty who had followed Sibald to Ely five only returned, to tell of months of dreary siege, a sudden night surprise, and a battle in which the last of the English leaders went down before the Norman spears.

Then came Hugo de Malines, younger son of a noble French family, who had followed William in search of plunder and had received as his reward the manor of Ellington, with all its rights and privileges. It was a valuable grant, for Ellington, though not large, was a wealthy little town, and capable of producing a good supply of riches for its lord.

At once Ellington was organized as a typical manor. No longer were the loose old English ways allowed. Every man's duties were set out clearly and enforced with rigour; indeed, but for the protection of the king's courts and the sheriff far more would have been exacted. The lord appointed a bailiff, or reeve, to supervise the work of the

54

villeins, while they had to choose one of their number as their own reeve, called the manor reeve, an unpopular official, whose duty it was to represent the villeins as a body, and who was rather in the position of a lance-corporal in the army, receiving kicks from superior and inferior alike, but no ha'pence from either. For if the villeins' tasks were ill done, on his devoted head descended the bailiff's wrath, while the villeins grumbled at his activities.

Of course, the folk of Ellington did not like it at all. In fact, they contemplated rebellion, but could never decide on a satisfactory plan. Ughtred, a tall, red-haired fellow, very sulky of aspect, tried to murder his lord, after having been fined in the manor court for failing to do his day's work on his lord's land. The promptness and efficiency with which he was hanged discouraged other would-be murderers. The old English courts had only imposed a fine for murder (the *wergild*). The vigour of this new rule surprised and disconcerted the English.

So, too, did the sudden rigour of the game-laws. It was not till Red Siward and Garth had lost their right hands for stealing the King's deer in the forest that lay close upon the manor of Ellington that the poaching zeal of its inhabitants cooled off.

These were unpleasant features of the new rule. Yet it had its advantages. If the King oppressed his people, at least he saw to it that nobody else did so. Especially did he clear the forests of outlaw gangs, and it became almost safe to do a day's journey over an English road, which certainly had not been the case under the feeble Edward the Confessor. Trade too began to expand in the new security.

Besides, the Normans were far more luxurious than the old English had ever been. They liked finer clothing, richer armour, more elaborate fittings to their houses, and gradually a little colony of foreign workmen began to collect in Ellington. There was, for example, Gilbert, a Flanders armour-smith, and a potter, Blaise of Rouen, who made curious ware very unlike the clumsy efforts of old Wulf, the local expert. Both these men married English girls, as did others like them, and began the development of a new race that had the solid qualities of the English mingled with the qualities of the more civilized races of the Continent.

Still, there was much grumbling, especially when Earl Hugo, who owned many other manors besides Ellington, settled upon that as his principal residence and set to work to build a castle, a great wooden affair on a raised mound of earth. The English swore and grumbled, but they dared do no more, for a grim body of foreign men-at-arms supervised the working gangs.

ONGAR CASTLE

This castle was built in the twelfth century upon the site of an earlier structure erected in the time of William I.

From a reconstruction by Charles H. Ashdown.

56

RYE CHURCH

A typical old English church, begun in Norman times and completed in the thirteenth century.

Photo F. Frith and Co., Ltd.

Under the Norman

But the town grew. The men-at-arms married and had families, strong, sturdy children of mixed blood, who began to develop new ideas and new methods. Still, the place remained largely agricultural in habits, but a steadily increasing body of traders, native and foreign, gathered under the grim castle mound.

This, then, led to a new development in the life of Ellington. For the Norman men-at-arms and the foreign craftsmen did not labour in the common fields along with the rest of the villagers. The latter, it is true, were entitled to board at their lord's table, but if any were married they needed to buy food, and even the single men sometimes spent what money they had on occasional country delicacies, as well as on ale and dice. The tradesmen increasingly, as their town work grew heavier, depended on others for their share of the food produced in the common fields.

But there were no grocers' shops, no butcher, no fruiterer to supply the needs of the town. It would be inconvenient for each man or his wife to go out into the country to seek for supplies. It was more convenient for those who had supplies to bring them into the town. So grew up the market, a day set aside each week when the folk from the outer fields came into the town with such produce as they could spare from their own needs to sell to the townsmen. Eggs, honey, vegetables from the tofts, that is, the little patches of garden ground that each man owned in addition to his share of the common fields, pigeons that the skilful fowlers among them had snared, chickens live or dead, these were offered in an open place in the centre of the town.

But the sellers and buyers alike were villeins, and owed dues to the lord of the manor, who therefore took a small toll from every user of the market. In return for this toll the earl appointed one to look after the market, settle disputes, and prevent cheating. This was the clerk of the market, and the first of whom we have any record was one Guy, a foreigner, probably a dependant of Roger de Malines, Hugo's grandson, who was then the lord of the manor.

He was a busy man, it would seem, from the list of his duties. It was Guy's business to check every weight and measure used in the market, to prevent brawls, to fix fair prices for various classes of goods, to prevent the use of bad money, to collect his lord's tolls, to seize and hold for punishment any thief or other disturber of the peace of the market.

Ellington was a growing town. Just about the end of William the Conqueror's reign, while the developments I have been describing were slowly taking place, a chance occurred to discover just

58

how it had grown. For there descended one day upon Ellington two learned clerks, servants of the distant King, who called before them the reeve of the manor and the four best men in it, that is the four richest villeins. These were then made to swear to tell the truth and ordered to answer certain questions.

"What was the extent of the manor of Ellington?"

"How many men dwelt upon it, and of what rank?"

" How many ploughs, oxen, cattle, sheep, swine, geese, and so on were there on the manor?"

" Whose was the manor in the time of Edward the Confessor? "

" Whose was it now? "

" What was its value in Edward's reign? "

" What was its value now?"

The answers to all these questions were written down in Domesday Book, and it was found that in Ellington, unlike many manors in England, there were more men and stock than formerly, and the estimate of its value was greater by five pounds, a large sum, than in the time of Edward. Certainly Ellington was a growing town.

Yet the life was still very much that of a village. There were Church Ales on saints' days, when everybody assembled at the church gate and sang and made merry, drinking a good deal of free

beer, but doing no harm. There were wet boon
days, when all the villagers had to turn to on the
lord's harvesting, but got their fill of good ale in
return for the extra work, there was the May Day
feast, and coarse jollity at Christmas, but nothing
elaborate. Even London Town had little more,
but there one might see minstrels or mountebanks,
unknown in remote Ellington.

The life of the village centred largely upon the
church. Not only were the individual members
baptised, married, and buried in or near its walls,
not only were the dead remembered in solemn
prayer, but the whole corporate life of the village
moved round the church. It was the Church that
provided such joys as they had, it was the Church
that gave what little education was provided;
often enough the meeting of the manor court was
held within the church garth. It was in the
church that the priest proclaimed to his congregation such orders from the king, as affected their
lives and happiness, it was to the church they
went to ease their souls of sorrow, or return thanks
for joy. Through the Church, and thus alone,
could a poor man rise to greatness. If we do not
understand this, the chronicles of the Middle Ages
are so much double Dutch to us of modern days.

It was to the Church that men turned for protection when **Count** Stephen of Boulogne, a good

man, but soft, and one that did no justice, became King Stephen of England. For this was the opportunity of the feudal baron, who had chafed for long under the stern rule of the Conqueror and his sons. And those barons hated the little towns that were becoming too independent.

So bands of savage raiders once again despoiled the land, and for the third time in its history Ellington was burned to the ground by a party under the savage Earl of Essex, Geoffrey de Mandeville. Further, old Ralph the goldsmith was seized by Earl Geoffrey, and when he would not tell where his store of gold lay the old man was crushed to death by being pressed into a sort of stone coffin full of sharp flints. Others suffered a like fate, and for a while Ellington was deserted.

But when the Conqueror's great-grandson, the second Henry, came to the throne a new day dawned for the town. Gone were the raiding barons, and a man might safely become rich, not fearing to lose his all as soon as he gained it. Not only that, Henry was more than King of England, he was lord of the sunny lands of South-western France as well, and a flourishing trade began to arise between those lands and England. For already the wool of the English sheep was beginning to be famous, soft, fine fleeces such as drier, harsher lands could not grow. Mercia and the

The English Town

East Midlands were by no means behindhand with their supply of wool, and there were cunning weavers in Flanders, whose duke was Henry's friend, who needed the clips of wool that England could supply.

So men began to trade on a larger scale. Good merchants of Ellington would buy up wool and send it off to Flanders, bringing back cargoes of goods such as Flanders supplied. As yet the trade was very small, but it would grow, and, as it grew, so would the town of Ellington.

The men of the town were freer too. It was the King's policy to help the towns, and to encourage them to secure as much freedom as possible. Also, with peace and security people were beginning to demand luxury, and luxuries can only be bought with money. The days when the lord of the manor was content to live on the products of his fields were passing; he desired fine wines from Bordeaux, fleet greyhounds from Spain, and his wife required tapestries and silks from Flanders and France. The old scheme by which unwilling villeins worked free upon their lord's fields produced bad work, sullenly done. So the lord of Ellington, Sir John Maline (the " de " had dropped in the course of years) called together his tenants and made, through his bailiff, for he spoke only Norman-French himself, a suggestion.

Under the Norman

"Why," said the bailiff, "should you swink and toil on my land for two or three days every week? Rather you shall pay twopence for each day's work that you owe and receive a copy of the manor roll with that agreement written fair upon it, so that nobody shall ever dispute your right to your land. Then with that money we will hire such of you as are poor and need a few extra pennies to work for my lord."

At first the people of Ellington grumbled. Twopence seemed a very great sum to pay, but they found that there was no help for it, and, once arranged, they found themselves freer than before, able to concentrate more on trade, and to work their own little holdings more easily than hitherto, so that soon they were earning such good money as not to feel the want of the twopences. Only those whom necessity compelled to hire themselves to the lord found that they had made a bad bargain, for now that he was paying for their labour the lord could and did punish slackness with loss of pay.

So when the great King died Ellington was ceasing to be a mere village, and was well on the way to become a prosperous and flourishing town, and the extravagant knight-errantry of the King's son, Richard Cœur-de-Lion, gave them an opportunity to take the next step in their progress.

63

CHAPTER V

Charter and Gild Merchant

RICHARD I was, as I have said, a knight-errant, typical of his age. Fighting he loved for its own sake, and an adventure like the Crusade, with plenty of fighting for a noble object, was the sort of thing to attract the Lion-heart. Within six months of coming to the throne Richard was sailing for Palestine. But Crusades cost money, and Richard was far from wealthy. He sold all he had, and certain things that were hardly his to sell, to raise the funds for his venture. So it was with most of his followers, and this was the opportunity for towns such as Ellington that desired their freedom.

The Gild of St Jude had grown powerful and important during the palmy days of Henry II. Some of the members were very wealthy men, but in strict law they were villeins still, having to pay their dues to the lord of the manor for their share of the common fields, and, in addition to that, dues when they sold cattle or sheep, married their sons and daughters, or carried out any business with strangers. Besides this, they must

64

grind their corn at the lord's mill, and pay him for the privilege.

So when the people of Ellington heard that their lord, William Malin, was going on crusade with the King, the alderman of St Jude's Gild, Thomas Gissing, called together the gildsmen and spoke to them thus :

" Brethren and sisters of the gild," he said, " for years we have longed to be free of the lord's bailiff and the continual payments that he demands, to-day a penny, to-morrow twopence. It seems to me that now we have a chance to secure our freedom."

There was a pause for a few moments.

" How ? " cried a score of voices.

" Thus," answered the alderman. " Let us go to the Earl and offer him a sum of money in return for a charter such as the citizens of London have demanded from the King, by which every freeman of this town shall have a share in appointing a mayor and alderman to rule us, and what we owe to the lord of the manor by way of dues for the land shall be compounded for by a sum to be raised by ourselves and paid each year over to the Earl, but by ourselves, not by his bailiff. Then the manor court will be in our hands, not the lord's, and we shall be free."

Gissing had travelled in France, where this

arrangement, called the Commune, was not unusual, and for many years had been seeking an
opportunity to obtain something of the sort in
his own town.

The gildsmen and women looked at each other;
it was a bold idea, but it might well be tried. So
a deputation was chosen to lay the townsmen's
request before the lord.

Earl William listened, and frowned slightly.
He had no sympathy with these townsfolk in
their desire for freedom, but the offer they made
was certainly attractive. He thought, with a
regretful sigh, of certain parts of France where
he would have needed to make no such concessions
to get some of their money from these wealthy
villeins, a little judicious torture would have done
all he required, but Henry Plantagenet had put a
decided end to that sort of thing in England, and
the money was certainly very badly needed. So,
with reluctance, a clerk was ordered to draw up a
charter such as the folk of Ellington desired, not
forgetting to bind them well down in the matter
of prompt payment of the promised annuity.

Thus Ellington became a borough. Every
freeman of the town should pay his share of the
annual tax, and, in return, should have a say in
choosing the mayor and aldermen who should
govern the town. But as the Gild of St Jude had

been mainly instrumental in securing the charter, it was further set down that to be a freeman of the town a man must belong to that gild or any other that might later be formed with the consent and approval of the town authorities. This was meant to prevent the town being ruled by mere weight of numbers should the poorer sort of the population increase too greatly. The gild naturally tended to grow more exclusive, especially when the next great change took place in its constitution, which will be spoken of later.

The first election of a mayor was a fine function. The 28th of October, the saint's day that commemorated the patron of gild and town alike, St Jude, was chosen as a fitting date, and on the morning of that day the whole town gathered outside the church gate. Then the alderman of the gild stood forth, and a clerk at his side read aloud the terms of the charter, in crabbed Latin, which Alderman Gissing, who had learned it off by heart the previous evening, translated to the crowd as the clerk read. Then somebody among the gildsmen suggested Gissing as a fit person to be the first mayor of Ellington and the rest cried loudly " A Gissing! A Gissing! "

Thus by the clamour of the excited crowd were chosen also twelve aldermen to help the mayor. There was Peter â Deane, John Custon, William the Miller, Gervaise Deholt, a foreign craftsman, Alaric Vernon, and others, men of wealth and standing in the town, mercers, and skilled craftsmen. It was a sign of the times. The old-fashioned folk who stuck to the fields and disliked the innovating traders (and there were such in Ellington) were not represented upon the council at all. Soon they were even more cut off from the life of the town.

Trade expanded rapidly, and more and more traders began to neglect the work of the fields, leaving that to poor, ignorant folk unfit for the life of trade and the subtleties of commerce. That meant that trade would require organization, just as the life of the farm was organized on the manor, and largely for the same reason, that no individual possessed enough capital to face unaided the changes and chances of trade.

For this purpose the Gild of St Jude, originally a charitable society, could easily be adapted. In the main its members were the traders of the town, who took risks that the ordinary peasant did not take, and therefore needed the protection of the gild more than they. The association was already something like an informal merchant gild. Very soon it developed into the real thing.

For no sooner was Ellington a chartered town, beginning to grow rich, than outside traders swarmed to the town to secure a share in its prosperity. But these outside traders could not be controlled as men born and dwelling in the town could be, and the good people of Ellington began to organize in self-defence.

"For," grumbled old Thomas Hatch, the leather-seller, " not only do these strangers wander to our town, taking the bread from the mouths of honest tradesmen by selling against them, but the saints alone know what sort of stuff they sell, and at what prices."

" Aye, indeed," agreed a crony, " but yesterday we ran out of town a rogue that was selling woollen cloth cheaper by a penny in the ell than we here can sell it, stuff that would tear if you but breathed on it, but there are fools enough that would buy to save their purses a penny or two, and honest men may go starve if they cannot sell good stuff as cheap as rogues sell shoddy."

So with grumbling and grutching was born the merchant gild of Ellington, and its first act was to decree that nobody who was not a member might trade retail within the town except in raw foods. It seems surprising to us that a mere trade body could so order the life of the town, but we must remember that the same men who were members of the gild were the freemen of the town, and entitled to make its laws and local regulations.

Thus the rules of the gild had all the force of the mayor and aldermen behind them.

Further, it was ordered that no member of the gild should be admitted without a seven years' apprenticeship unless a stranger from another town settled in Ellington, who could produce from the authorities of his former residence a certificate that he had served a proper apprenticeship and was skilled at his trade. This was necessary, because the gild went on to lay down strict rules as to how trade was to be carried on.

Fair prices were to be fixed for every article, and no member of the gild was to take more or less than that price. Quality also was regulated, all goods had to come up to a certain standard, and he who sold goods of baser quality would be severely punished. Lending or borrowing money at interest was strictly forbidden, as also was going into partnership with a stranger.

All this meant that Ellington would be a close town, where outsiders might not trade unless wholesale merchants, men who brought foreign goods to sell in bulk to members of the Ellington gild. On the whole the scheme was good for trade ; without some such protection the trade of England would have been at the mercy of unskilful fools and cheating knaves, for there was no police force except the town constable, a mere

A Fourteenth-century Street at Newcastle-on-Tyne

70

The Marlipins, Shoreham-by-Sea

This picturesque old building, one of the few remaining of Norman date devoted from the first to civic or secular purposes, was erected in the twelfth century, the facing of Caen stone and knapped flints being added two hundred years later. It was probably used in connexion with the business of what was then a flourishing seaport, and the family of de Braose, the lords of the manor, may have built it as a sort of clearing-house and storeroom for the dues which they claimed from all ships casting anchor in the harbour and all merchants frequenting the market. These dues were often paid in kind instead of in money, and would include casks of wine, bales of cloth or hides, and barrels of spices. Though it is not known for certain whether this building was used as a meeting-place by the members of the local craft gilds and fraternities, it may be regarded as typical of the halls where they were wont to meet between Norman times and the Reformation.

Photo A. J. R. Chambers, Shoreham-by-Sea

thief-catcher, chosen for brawn rather than brain, and a street watch at night, which was provided by the citizens, taking turns to patrol the streets after dark. The rogue or incompetent fool, therefore, could have worked his will on English trade but for the strict rules of the traders themselves designed to prevent it.

But for the rest of the people of Ellington—the farming class, the unskilled labourers, porters, odd-job men—a growing population, it was not so satisfactory. It meant that these people, though they lived in the town and had to obey its laws, were at the mercy of the richer men, since not being freemen of the gild they had no vote, and not having the money to become apprentice to some freeman, who, of course, expected a premium in return for teaching a boy his trade, they had no chance of getting votes.

At first this did not seem a serious matter. The population of casual labourers was not large, for there was not much demand for them in the early days before trade became as important and extensive as it did later on. But it increased steadily, for as years went by the old manor system tended to break up. Men grew discontented on old-fashioned manors where the lord refused to accept payment instead of labour, and when they could they ran away. But it was no use running to another manor, so the runaway serf made for the nearest town, to lose himself in its streets and alleys, for it was one of the most cherished privileges of the chartered town that any man who had lived within its boundaries for a year and a day could never be claimed again by his lord. He was free. But that did not mean that he was free of the town. He might live within its walls, but he might not, unless by some chance he could secure the money to serve his apprenticeship, trade within its boundaries. So the escaped serf became a mere casual, living on what chance odd jobs would bring him, and a great deal of bitterness arose between these unprivileged townsmen and the gildsmen with their exclusive rights.

Thus the number dwelling in Ellington increased, till the town lost all semblance to the village that had once stood in the forest by the ford. Let us look at it now, when the grant of a charter has confirmed its position as an important and growing town.

It lies on a slight rise above the level of the surrounding fields, a huddle of houses clustering round the lord's castle, for a Malin still lives in Ellington Castle, and his custom and that of the garrison that holds the castle under him for the king is still the mainstay of many of the traders of the town below. The streets are incredibly narrow and twisted, partly because houses have been built anywhere and anyhow, partly because such narrow, twisted streets are useful in case of attack, they are difficult for an enemy to penetrate. The condition of those streets would turn the foulest denizen of a modern slum sick. Drainage there is none, if anyone had slops or dirty water he simply emptied them from the window of his house, having first yelled a warning to any chance wayfarer below.

For water the river suffices, or one or two wells that have been dug to supply that part of the town farthest from the river. But those wells are the usual receptacles for unwanted kittens, dead dogs, old useless shoes or other articles of attire, and, since it is the easiest method, housewives washing their clothes do so at the well-side, and the dirty water drains into the well. On the whole it is not surprising that typhoid, typhus, plague, smallpox, and every other filth-disease decimate the town at intervals, as the traveller may see if he goes to the church.

This lies below the castle mound, not the old wooden affair of Saxon times, but a fine stone building, still not quite complete. The church has been built with money left by pious and charitable citizens, and, I fear, by rogues as well, who, contemplating the unpleasant future promised by the

The English Town

Church for such as they, have adopted this form of fire insurance. Here you may see monuments carved in stone to the memory of benefactors and others. There is a fine high altar, dedicated to St Mary the Virgin, and in little chapels to the north and south of that altar other smaller ones, dedicated to various saints, usually built and endowed by somebody on condition that their souls shall be prayed for there. Candles burn round the altars. Altogether a church worthy of the town and its founders.

Look now at the houses. The better sort are perhaps two storeys high. Downstairs is the general living-room, kitchen and dining-room all in one, with perhaps a store-room at the side. In front of the house is a low wooden booth, the shop where the goods are sold that the householder deals in. Behind, perhaps a warehouse and factory, for all these goods are made on the premises by master and apprentices. Here, in the common living-rooms, sleep the apprentices and servants. Above stairs may be a single bare chamber, where the master of the house and his family sleep. The house is of wood, ill built and draughty, and there is no glass in the windows, but great wooden shutters can be barred at night to keep out the cold night air that our ancestors were convinced led to unnumbered ills.

74

Charter and Gild Merchant

Such would be the home of a wealthy and well-respected man, mayor, perhaps, of his town.

For the poorer folk there was no such luxury as this. A mere hovel, little if any better than the wattle-and-daub huts of the Britons who had once dwelt on this spot, perhaps with a dismal yard around it where a few scraggy fowls picked a living, and in that hovel one or two families existed rather than lived. The only point where these folk were better off than modern slum-dwellers was that they lived and worked for the most part out of doors, and therefore would not suffer as a modern indoor worker would living in such a hole.

But if they were dirty and ill-planned and full of crazy houses, the streets of Ellington were at least picturesque. Few people could either read or write, and it was, therefore, of little use for the tradesman to inscribe his name and trade above his door. Thus, picture signs, large and gaily coloured, creaked above the narrow alleys of the town to show the trades followed by its inhabitants. Perhaps a golden boot would mark the shoemaker's shop, the sign of the " Coffin and Cradle " his whose work it was to make both for those who needed them, and a gaily coloured bolt of cloth represented the home of the cloth mercer. Perhaps, if the shopkeeper's name lent itself to the plan, it too would be represented by a picture;

for instance, a man named Fisher might have a crude picture of an angler hauling in his catch painted above his shop, together with the sign of his trade.

Such was the medieval town, picturesque, insanitary, unsafe after sundown, straggling higgledy-piggledy around the church. Later, perhaps, someone would build a gildhall, or clothhall, where the gildsmen and the mayor and corporation might hold their meetings instead of in the church itself. But except for this the appearance of the ordinary medieval town changed little till Tudor times, and this description of my town of Ellington must serve till we come to days when new discoveries and ideas bring about changes, not only in the life, but in the outward appearance of the town.

CHAPTER VI
Changes and Chances

THE reigns of John and Henry III brought their troubles for England, but the towns were not so greatly stirred by the events that take up so many pages in our history books as one might expect.

John's reign is, of course, famous for the Great Charter, yet it would be difficult to see in what way that document, of which so much is made, affected the lives of the good burgesses of Ellington. The freedom from taxation without their own consent, the right to trial by their peers, which, incidentally, does not mean trial by jury, these affected the great barons. True the barons promised to pass on to their men the privileges that the King gave to them, but they do not appear to have done so.

In truth, the Charter, had it ever been carried out, would have given rise to serious trouble with the towns. In one clause John promises that foreign merchants shall trade freely in England, and in another that London and chartered towns shall have their privileges unimpaired. But the most cherished of all the privileges of the chartered towns was just this, that foreign merchants should *not* be allowed freedom of trade within their boundaries, and how the compilers of the Charter meant to combine these two opposite promises is by no means clear.

On the whole the sympathies of Ellington were with King John. He may have been a brute and a tyrant, but he was far away and did not trouble the townsfolk much. On the other hand, Earl Malin was one of the barons of the Charter, and the citizens had a pretty shrewd idea what would happen to their privileges should the great barons break down the despotism that the Norman and Angevin kings had built up in England. So we find that when John called out his followers and attacked the barons the East Country towns, such as King's Lynn, were inclined to his rather than to his enemies' side.

More especially was this the case when the barons called in French aid. The towns of England were extremely exclusive; in Ellington, for example, a Nottingham man only a few miles away would be called a foreigner. That form of patriotism, an elementary and crude form, that consists in disliking foreigners simply because they are foreigners, was growing in English towns when it existed nowhere else. For the foreigner came into competition with the English townsman, and was accordingly disliked.

It is this that explains the attitude of Ellington

in the next national crisis, the quarrel between Simon de Montfort and King Henry III. For Earl Simon announced his intention of clearing all foreigners out of England, conveniently forgetting to mention that he was one himself, and the towns of England responded to the cry. Listen to the gossip in an alehouse in one of Ellington's narrow streets.

"Aye," growls one portly merchant, "a curse on all foreigners, I say. Lands and money and good posts, all must be given to men of Poitu and Savoy, and Englishmen swink and save to fill their pockets. I'm for Earl Simon."

"And I," cried a thin, reedy voice. It was Gerald le Clerk, a doctor and lawyer who was in minor orders—that is, he was neither priest nor deacon, and had no intention of being either, but he held minor rank among the clergy, rank that did not prevent him from marrying and earning a living, which he did by practising one of the learned professions.

"Why so, Master Clerk?" asked a surprised burgess. "I thought that you of the Church were all for our pious King Henry."

"Piety's well enough," the other replied tartly, "but see, I must pay a penny here, and twopence there, this for a tax to the Holy Father, God bless him, this to pay for the war against Sicily that his Holiness has engaged in, this for a special levy to fight the Saracen, so that when all is paid I've scarce a penny to my name."

A tall, gaunt man, who had sat apart from the gossips, outside the actual door of the alehouse, indeed, in the porch, joined the conversation. He was a friar, one of the new preachers who had come to England, and of whom there will be more to tell.

" You are right, friends," he said, his voice hoarse and earnest. " Sir Simon is the man for England, who will have no more loafing monks from Italy made bishops in England to reward their idle trickery."

Men shook their heads at that, for they knew how deep was the hatred between the friars and the monks. But most considered that the friar had gone too far; their own monks of Ellington Abbey were neither stupid nor idle, and on the whole were liked and respected by the townsmen. But nobody cared to contradict the fierce-eyed friar, whom all regarded with superstitious awe.

So, when Simon de Montfort governed England, Ellington was among those boroughs that sent two representatives to his new sort of Parliament.

There was much talk about that in the streets and inns of Ellington. It looked as if Earl Simon meant to revive the old Norman and Plantagenet policy of using the lesser folk to check the great barons. For when he called his Parliament he sent not only for the great barons. There were many smaller knights entitled to go to the King's council, men who held freehold land direct from the King, but who usually could not afford the expense of journeying to council. So de Montfort suggested that all freeholders in each shire should meet and elect two of their number to represent them, so that by dividing the cost among all the smaller sort of men could get their opinions heard. But a chartered town was a freeholder too, it held land, and was expected to supply military service, or money in lieu, to the King, just as a knight or baron was expected to do. So they, too, were to be represented.

But de Montfort quarrelled with barons and smaller folk alike, for he was a hard, proud man, insanely fond of his useless and greedy sons, and soon the people of Ellington, or their leaders—for the people themselves had little political knowledge—decided that Edward the Prince was the man for them. One thing especially that de Montfort did contributed to this : he allied himself with the Welsh.

"A shame and a scandal," cried Geoffry Pauncefot, the Mayor of Ellington, when word came to the town that de Montfort had made a treaty with Llewellyn of Wales, "for are not these Welshmen foreigners too, aye, and wild

F

savage wretches, worse than any that were King
Harry's friends? "

So when Lord Edward beat and killed de
Montfort at the battle of Evesham, and took over
in his father's name the rule of England, even
those who had loved and supported de Montfort,
deeming that his objects were good, heaved a sigh
of relief. There was peace at last, and the people
of Ellington could settle down to increase their
prosperity.

Things were moving in England, slowly but
surely. A sudden new wave of religious energy
came storming up from the south, the grim, black
friars of St Dominic, the gentle grey-robed
Franciscans, teaching and preaching, building
schools and hospitals, experimenting in new
things. Was not one of them, Roger Bacon,
imprisoned on suspicion of witchcraft for his bold
speculations, and blowing new life into dead old
things? The commercial life of the country
answered to the religious. Men set out to do new
things, and trade began to be less local, more
important in the life of the country.

It is probably to these friars that Ellington
owes its grammar school, that has bred famous
men in its time. True, the school is said to have
been founded by King Edward VI, but, as with
many another foundation that bears the boy-king's

BOYS IN SCHOOL AND A BOY BEING BIRCHED

From a mid-fourteenth-century encyclopaedia of Canon Law in the British Museum.

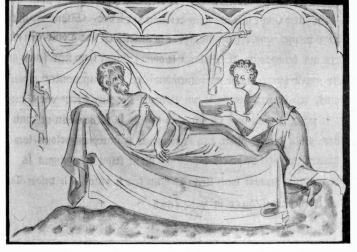

Isaac blessing Jacob

This miniature shows the bed of the period, with curtain suspended from a rod, the absence of night-clothes, and the characteristic arrangement of hair and beard.

From Queen Mary's Psalter, early fourteenth century.

83

Changes and Chances

name, all that the sickly Tudor did was to save from the wreck of the Dissolution an old foundation, and refound it under his own name. Certainly there was a school in Ellington from the early Middle Ages, and certainly friars taught in it.

One cannot, however, say that the teaching would commend itself to modern ideas, whether the ideas of masters or of boys. The hours were long, the subjects curious. Six in summer, seven in winter were the hours of opening, at five and four in the afternoon school ended. The subjects were few and dull. Small boys learned to read and write and do simple arithmetic. Probably if they were not intended for the Church, that was as far as they went. But those who meant to go on to take orders, whether to become clergymen or to adopt such professions as lawyer, doctor, or schoolmaster (most of whom in those days were clergymen of a sort), had to go on to far harder things. They had to learn Latin to a very high standard, rhetoric—that is, the art of public speaking (one wishes that budding clergymen were still taught this subject)—and logic, the art of arguing. Examinations consisted of a curious ceremony, boys would learn up certain subjects, and argue publicly upon them.

Punishments were ferocious, the usual being a

huge birch or heavy leather whip, and thirty or forty lashes no uncommon penalty for a slip in translation or grammar. But there were the saints' days to make up for it. Then there was a holiday, and the boys amused themselves. We do not know whether Ellington school had the curious custom that existed in some schools: that on certain holidays the boys came to school each with his cock, and the master organized cock-fighting in the schoolroom, and gave a prize to the owner of the winning cock.

The school was a great boon to the town, for if a poor boy were clever and promising the school would educate him free and enable him to become a clergyman. That was a great thing for him, for otherwise there was scarcely any chance of a poor boy rising from the rank in which he had been born. We know of a Bishop Ellington—a clergyman on ordination used to take a new name, usually that of his birthplace (for example, Archbishop Peckham)—and this bishop speaks of having been a poor boy and taught free of charge by the good friars of his town, which, as I have explained, was probably Ellington, and the school of which he speaks that which I have described.

But for the wealthy folk also the school did yeoman service. It would take the sons of traders and teach them what they needed to know to carry on their fathers' business. Thus there grew up in Ellington, as in other towns, a number of men who were not clergymen, but who could read and write, so that if any of them wanted to learn more they knew how to begin. All over England this was happening, and it is the first faint beginning of the movement that we call the Renaissance, the rediscovery of old, lost knowledge and its application to daily life. There will be more to tell of this in a later chapter.

So began the long reign of the first Edward, a time of growing prosperity for Ellington. For Edward found it to his benefit to ally with the Flanders folk, and the demand for English wool increased. Soon by the muddy water of the river there grew up a harbour and ship-building dock, and Ellington ships nosed their way up the muddy harbours of Flanders laden with bales of fine English wool, and beat back against the westerly winds with cargoes of made-up cloth from the famous Flanders looms. Sometimes they brought other things, strange Eastern spices and silks, for these too were to be had in Flanders, having been brought there by long weary journeys, first by camel from the far lands beyond the sunrise down to the Mediterranean shore, thence by

The English Town

galley to Venice, the greatest seaport of the day, and thence by pack-pony and river-boat over the passes and up the wide Rhine river to Flanders at its mouth, whence they were distributed over northern Europe. Ellington began to grow rich ; its chief citizens were no longer content with simple homespuns, and fine, furred gowns might be seen in its streets, so fine that soon we have laws made by the King against such ostentation, laws that failed to effect their purpose.

Fishing, too, had grown steadily as an industry in Ellington. The cold North Sea swarmed with fish, and there were many, many Christian fast-days when meat might not be eaten. It paid, therefore, to catch and salt great quantities of fish to send inland, where they were in great demand. The stink of drying fish and rotting offal fouled the air around the growing harbour by the river-bank.

Then came the Scottish and Welsh wars. They had little effect upon the town of Ellington, though they gave the citizens a chance to cheer their King as he came marching through, six feet six inches in height, handsome, debonair—a man to stir the heart of man or woman. A few of the younger sparks in the town could not resist the glamour of the marching men, and those of them that returned had strange tales to tell of wild, cold lands to the north and wild, fierce people ; also of a new weapon they had seen, and perhaps learned to use, a terrible bow, six feet in length, that would shoot its arrow a full two furlongs.

Far more important to the life of the town than Edward's wars were the laws that he made, for these brought a measure of security hitherto unknown. Strict regulations were made as to the keeping clear of the roads, all brushwood to be cut down for a certain distance on each side of the way, so that robbers should not conceal themselves therein. But laws like that had been made before. Edward did something else ; he appointed keepers of the peace, men specially appointed to see that these things were done. He ordered that when a thief was chased he should be followed till caught; the chase must not be given up, as had been the custom, when the sheriff or constable reached the border of his own district. That meant that merchantmen could travel over the roads with greater safety, and thus trade increased.

There was another law, too, that had great effects. That was the statute called *Quia Emptores*, which allowed the sale of feudal land, but on condition that a man who bought feudal land became responsible for the duties attached, not to the man from whom he bought the land, but to that man's overlord. That made possible something new.

For instance, Roger Wainwright, growing rich on the proceeds of his craft, bought from Earl Simon Malin a parcel of land on which to build a new house for himself. But this land owed service to the king, and its owner must be prepared to supply one armed knight in time of war. This duty now fell to the Wainwright, who thus became a freeman, a gentleman, in fact. A new road was opened up by which a man could rise to higher rank. The successful trader might aspire to become something more, as, in the reign of Edward's grandson, one Michael de la Pole, a merchant of Kingston-upon-Hull, did, becoming Earl of Suffolk. The rigid class distinctions of feudal days were wearing thinner.

The same effect was produced by Edward's famous Parliament of 1295 ; probably that was the King's motive, or one of his motives, in calling the assembly. Here baron and plain citizen met to discuss the affairs of the nation, and to bring to the King's notice their grievances and desires. There was the matter of the sheriff of Lincoln, for example, who had tried to interfere with the privileges of Ellington town and arrest a criminal who had escaped from his county and taken refuge in Ellington. Master John Gaster, the burgess sent to represent Ellington, brought this up in Parliament. But here Master Gaster found himself in hot water. The King received the petition that he was commanded to bear to his Court, read it and frowned.

" And why, good sir," asked the King, " was this notorious rogue allowed to run loose in your town ; why did you not try to hang him yourselves if you are so eager to keep your privileges of justice ? "

Master Gaster looked sheepish and shuffled his feet.

" Know," stormed the King, " that not London Town itself is privileged to break my laws. By the splendour of God, you shall not keep your town as a refuge for escaping rogues, and had best tell your mayor as much if he wants to remain mayor ! "

After that, was discussed the matter of taxes to be payed to enable the King to deal with the Scottish rebels, and, having cut these down as low as they could, the Parliament-men jogged off home, Master Gaster with a rebuke that he proposed to pass on to the mayor at the first opportunity.

So came the troubled days of Edward II, and of the infamous Earl Richard Malin, who took personal part in the brutal murder of that unfortunate King. But from his evil deed good came to Ellington, as you shall see.

CHAPTER VII
The Fair

EARL RICHARD MALIN lay dying, a terrible fear in his heart, a terrible sound in his ears—the screams of a man dying by torture in a gloomy dungeon, and that man his liege-lord and King, murdered by order of his faithless wife. Life had been well enough for Earl Richard, plenty of wine and fighting and brutal pleasure, but now came the end. The priest who stood by his side watched with grave face the eyes of the dying man. What consolation had the Church for such as he?

"Pray for my soul! Pray for my soul!" screamed the terrified Earl.

"I will pray, my son," answered the priest's grave voice, "but what of the future when my poor voice is stilled?"

For a moment the man on the bed lay silent. How should he make sure that throughout all ages the voice of the priest should be lifted at Mass for the repose of his guilty soul? Then:

"A fair, good Father; I will grant to the town of Ellington an annual fair, and all men shall come

The Fair

to it free of the tolls that strangers used to pay to me before they might buy or sell on my liberties without the walls. Then such dues as are paid shall go to your abbey so that prayers may be said for my soul."

The priest nodded.

" I will have the charter amended and brought to you to sign," he said.

For it must be remembered that when a lord granted a charter to a town he granted only what was written in it. Other rights and privileges, not mentioned in the charter, remained with the grantor. Now, though Earl William in Richard I's reign had granted many things to the town of Ellington, he had retained the right to levy toll outside the town gates upon stranger merchants.

So the charter was amended. Ellington was to have a fair, three days in each year, when strangers from all over England might enter the town free of toll, and, on paying a small tax to the Abbot of St Jude's Abbey, trade freely in the space of ground set apart for the fair within the lord's demesne outside the town. Meanwhile, the shops in Ellington town, except those that sold provisions and other necessities, were to remain closed.

This meant a great boon to the traders of Ellington. For until the fair had been established they could never know when they might be able to secure such goods as could not easily be got near at hand—Flanders cloth and Eastern goods and so forth. Now they could depend upon three days in the year when these goods were to be exposed near their own town shops, and a man might lay in his stock for the year without going outside his own town. Others would come too, men from small inland towns, to buy at Ellington Fair, and their coming would be profitable to the good citizens of Ellington who must lodge and feed them for the days of the fair.

It is a strange sight, the fair-ground of Ellington, on the morning of the opening of the first fair. The ground just without the town boundary is like the camping ground of a beggar's army, full of little tents and booths of every shape and colour. Merchants in cloth and velvet jostle ragged beggars and fantastically clad mountebanks and jugglers, and all crowd expectantly toward the centre of the fair-ground, where stands a fat man in a long black gown, steward of the Abbey of St Jude, whose duty it is to supervise the doings of the fair. Two beadles stand beside him, and as the moment approaches for the opening of the fair they cry for silence. The crowd hushes its chatter.

Then in a rapid, sing-song tone the steward reads the charter that is the authority for holding the fair, finishing by a command to all men to keep

The Fair

the peace of the fair and deal justly. The fair is open, and the merchants hurry back to their booths, the jugglers and public entertainers to their stands.

Babel breaks out within the fair-ground of Ellington:

" Fine velvet of Bruges! " yells one brazen-lunged apprentice. " Come buy. Come buy. Come buy! "

" What d'ye lack? " howls a rival. " Good silks and laces, all good, cheap! "

A hundred other young voices join the clamour, each doing its best to drown that of its neighbour, and up and down the noisy alleys wander the would-be buyers.

" How much the ell? " asks one, fingering a piece of cloth. The seller names his price. Shrugging contemptuously, the buyer turns away.

" Am I made of pure gold, think you? " he asks sarcastically.

This is all part of the game. The seller lowers his demand, the buyer raises his offer, till a price is reached, higher or lower according to the state of the market, that one will give and the other take. The piece changes hands, and another would-be buyer approaches to begin again the weary bargaining by which a price is settled.

Round the border of the actual fair are other

The English Town

booths and raised stages. This is where the parasites, who always haunted these institutions, carry on their business.

Here is a man in a furred velvet robe, very dirty and torn, but it looks impressive enough compared with the rough, hodden grey clothes of the people around him.

" Good masters and dames," he is saying, " here am I, Giovanni Sampeti, from Bologna." Bologna was the greatest university of its day. " I will draw both teeth and stumps without pain, and without damage to your mouths."

A trembling youth, heavily bribed by Giovanni, whose real name is plain John Samp, and who has never been nearer Bologna than Southampton town, climbs on to the rough stage. With heroic fortitude he conceals his agony as the dentist wrenches at his jaw. At last the self-styled Giovanni holds up a bloodstained tooth.

" Now, sir, there was no pain, I'll warrant you."

" Why, I scarce knew it was out," stutters the youth, choking back his agony. The silver penny that the dentist has promised him is worth some discomfort to earn.

The sufferers from toothache in the crowd below gained confidence, and soon the dentist is driving a roaring trade, ' roaring ' in more senses than one.

94

The Fair

Nearby stands another, dressed in the habit of a palmer, a pilgrim to the Holy Land. He sells with raucous shouting a number of medicines warranted to cure every disease under the sun, with many jeers at his dentist rival.

" See," he yells, " the fellow would wrench the milk teeth from a babe's mouth. He has no skill of medicines to heal and soothe. Now I, I will sell you, and all for one farthing, a packet of simples that you shall place upon the aching tooth, and repeat certain holy words that I shall teach you, all for nothing, and the pain shall straightway vanish. Or, if you be troubled with pains in the midriff, why, I have here a decoction of herbs gathered in Palestine, where Our Lord suffered, aye, from under the very shadow of His Holy Cross, that shall cure all your ills." And so on.

A bigger rogue this than the sham dentist, who at least does not try to play upon the religious feelings of the people.

Farther along is a juggler, who tumbles quaintly and twists his supple body into queer shapes, then throws high into the air his gilt balls, catching them as they spin with amazing ease and dexterity —a popular fellow. Farther on is an enclosure where now two cocks are fighting furiously, cheered on by excited groups of supporters on both sides. To-night there will be even greater excitement—when a poor brute of a bull is baited by savage dogs.

There is a commotion in the centre of the ground. Some poor rascal has been caught stealing from a booth. The steward sits in a booth surmounted by the arms of the Abbey, and before him the man is brought.

This is the Court of Pie Powder (*pieds poudrés*, " dusty feet "), the swiftest and most terrible court in England, held only in fair-time, when quick, stern justice is needed, quicker than the ordinary courts can supply. There can be no doubt of the fellow's guilt, and he is dragged off. We shall see him again if we leave the fair by the main entrance, a bundle of ragged clothes swinging in the wind, a warning to thieves and cutpurses like him to keep clear of the fair-ground.

Now comes another case, not a serious one according to certain modern ideas, at least the offence for which this man is dragged before the court is one frequently committed by modern advertisers. He has sold false top samples—that is, created a demand by selling a few excellent articles, and then selling shoddy when the first report of the good, cheap stuff to be got had attracted customers.

" To stand in the pillory till sundown," is the

PUBLIC ENTERTAINERS
From a manuscript in the British Museum.

THE BATTLE OF SLUYS

This interesting picture from an old manuscript shows the English and French ships
grappling each other—a feature of naval warfare in those early days.

97

sentence of the court, and the swindler is fixed in that machine, his head through one hole, his arms through two others. Here he remains, the target for varied missiles from the mob, rotten vegetables, dead cats, and sometimes heavier objects, jagged pieces of brickbat, or stone jars.

Lastly comes a case between a French merchant and an English, a complicated matter, needing careful attention. For the French merchant will not like to have the case judged by English law, and the English merchant will refuse to accept the French point of view. So the steward decides the case by ' law merchant,' which is the same all over Europe, specially designed for dealing with mercantile disputes.

Such was Ellington Fair—typical of the fairs of medieval England, which were most important features of English life, for it was at the fairs that most of the trade of the country was carried on, especially the foreign trade that was daily growing more important.

We have now arrived at the period of the Hundred Years' War, a period of the utmost importance for Ellington as for other towns in England. For the Hundred Years' War, at least till 1360, is no mere struggle for the crown of France, as is often suggested. It is something far deeper than that ; and one of the questions to

G

be fought out was certainly the existence and prosperity of English trade, and therefore of the English towns.

For by this time the wool trade was becoming the staple trade of England. There were wide spaces that would bear sheep but not the plough, and owners of such lands were beginning to use them for sheep-rearing instead of letting them run waste. This was especially true of the monks, always to the fore in the development of agriculture, simply because they had at their disposal the records of the classical world of Rome, and many treatises on agriculture in Latin, which they could study to the profit of their own farms.

Now there were two great markets for English wool, Flanders and the English duchy of Bordeaux in South France, whence made-up goods and wine were exported to England. But the new King of France, Philip of Valois, was trying to get both these territories (Flanders was an independent province) under his strong control, and if he did he could at any time ruin the English wool trade by stopping trade with these two places.

Also, the Channel was rendered unsafe by Norman pirates, and there was continual trouble between them and English sailors. Imagine if you can the feelings of the people of Ellington when, helpless to go to her aid, for the wind was contrary, they saw far away to the eastward the glare of a burning ship, and guessed that it must be the *Holy Maid*, belonging to Master Graver, a citizen of their town, and heard later from a chance survivor how the *Holy Maid* had been set upon, gutted, and burned by a pirate ship not five miles off shore.

Can it be wondered at then that when King Edward III declared himself Lord of the Narrow Seas, and allied himself with that party in Flanders which was opposing the French, the citizens of Ellington supported him? They even forgot their habitual thrift and instructed their representative in Parliament to vote for a large tax for the purposes of the war. For the King's supposed claim to the French throne they cared nothing—it was something to shout about, no more—but these other matters were serious.

So till 1360 the folk of Ellington were all for the war. Not only was it being fought for their safety, it brought wealth to the town, for men who had won great ransoms and secured great plunder in war were willing enough to spend it when they returned on silks and satins for their wives and fine velvet clothes for themselves, or rare and curious wines, all of which the merchants of Ellington could supply with more ease when the Battle of Sluys cleared the sea for England, making trade and commerce safer than ever before.

But when, after the successful Creçy and Poitiers campaigns and the treaty of Brétigny that gave England all she could in reason demand, the insane pride of the Black Prince and John of Gaunt forced on war again, the opinion of the folk of Ellington changed very considerably. For one thing they could see no good in the war, and grudged paying taxes to support it; for another it was now a losing war, and neither ransom nor loot are to be won in losing campaigns. It was all paying out, but no paying in. The folk of Ellington grumbled furiously as the old King sank into decrepitude and the land was ruled by the quarrelsome Black Prince and John of Gaunt.

Then there was the trouble with Master Wyclif, who stirred the country with his preaching, crying that monks and clergy should be poor for the love of Christ, not owners of a fifth of the land of England and the best fifth at that.

Whereat the wise, and I fear greedy, burgesses of Ellington nodded their heads. Some, it is true, agreed with Wyclif from religious motives, forgetting that if Church land was so rich it was the industry and skill of the monks that made it so, for often that rich land had been poor, useless soil when the monks first received it. Others agreed with Wyclif from motives of envy; they wanted to share out the riches of the Church among themselves.

Then John of Gaunt took up Wyclif's cause, because he too wanted a share of the lands of the Church if any were to be had, and the Black Prince opposed him out of mere contrariety and supported the orthodox Church party, and Ellington was split into three groups: those who supported the Black Prince, those who supported John, and those who cried " A plague on both your houses," and wanted peace and prosperity, but could find no leader in England who offered those wares.

Then Wyclif produced a daring heresy, attacking the teaching, not the wealth, of the Church, and most of his supporters dropped him as if he had been a hot brick, and England split itself again into those who wanted the war to go on, and those who wanted peace, so that heads were broken in Ellington streets by rival factions, and all the town was in a turmoil.

And then, after the awful disease known as the Black Death, of which the next chapter treats, and all these squabbles and riots, came the poll-tax and disaster.

CHAPTER VIII

"*From Battle and Murder, and from Sudden Death*"

ONE day in the year 1349 you might have seen a crowd hurrying toward the parish church of Ellington, and remarked upon their appearance. Men, women, and children herded toward the church, with white, set faces and terrified eyes, looking askance at each other, as if each feared his neighbour.

That indeed was the case, for terrible news had spread round the town, whispered in awed tones first here then there, and the listener's face blanched and his hands trembled as he heard the tale.

" It has come! It has come! "

The Black Death was among them, that terrible scourge that spread up from the South of England, creeping like the relentless tide over city and village alike, till there was not a town in England that had not been plunged into the bitter waters of death. What it was, this awful sickness, we do not know. Probably it was the bubonic plague, a frightful disease that still takes its toll of human life in India and the East, and is sometimes seen in or near docks in England where come ships from countries in which the plague rages. Some modern doctors have suggested that the Black Death was a terrible epidemic of influenza such as swept over England in 1919, and of course this is possible.

Whatever it was, the people of Ellington had good reason for their terror, for there were towns in England which suffered so that never again did they rise above the position of mere villages, and others that simply vanished, all their inhabitants dead or fled for safety.

And now it was among them. Last night Peter the Shoemaker, living in East Wall Street, had complained of pain and discomfort; this morning he was dead. No man seeing the body could doubt of what disease he had died. By to-night God knew how many might have gone the same way.

" From plague, pestilence, and famine; from battle and murder, and from sudden death,

" *Good Lord, deliver us.*"

Petition and response were chanted in sing-song Latin, but the hearts of all the worshippers were in the cry. They had all these things to fear.

For as the plague spread the town went mad. Law and order vanished; there was none to enforce the law, and if there had been the harshest judge would scarcely care to imprison a criminal, however vile, when imprisonment meant sentence of death by the awful Black Plague. Apprentices whose masters were dead, and who therefore had no livelihood, workmen in the same position, men of wealth and station who had lost all in the utter stagnation of trade that the plague brought, joined themselves in gangs and lived by highway robbery. Dead men lay unburied in the streets, the air was foul beyond even its normal foulness, the aspect of the town deserted and awful. Men who escaped the pest went mad with the dreadfulness of the place. Those who could fled into the country, where many starved in ditches, for the land was untilled and desolate, offering no sustenance to the fugitives from the towns.

The height of the plague came, and the streets of Ellington were deserted. Only the tall forms of half a dozen Grey Friars strode from house to house, nursing the sick, tending the dying, praying with the fearful, comforting the bereaved. Brave men these, for they were doomed to death and knew it. Did they but know it their order was doomed as well, for it was after the terrible destruction of this plague that such men as Chaucer's friar, who was " the best beggar in his house," came to fill up the ranks of the wanderers, and brought discredit on a great movement.

From Sudden Death

So at last the terrible pestilence passed, and Ellington woke again from that nightmare sleep, but it was a different and saddened town. Familiar faces had vanished, and those that were left were different men, grey-faced, weary, old. The very children seemed to have the weight of centuries upon their shoulders.

Then came the famine to complete the work of the plague. For the manors lying in the country round, whence the townsfolk of Ellington had drawn most of their supplies—most of the people of the town having ceased now to support themselves in the matter of food—had lain untilled while the Death worked its will on lord and villein alike. Food was scarce and dear, and many who had escaped the plague fell victims to the famine. Men said that the end of all things was at hand. Wild priests, men driven mad by the horrors they had seen, stalked up and down the land, proclaiming that the end of the world had come, quoting passages from Daniel and Revelations in support of their ideas, proposing the most fantastic schemes of salvation. Men and women wandered the roads of England flogging themselves and each other almost to death in their religious frenzy, monasteries and abbeys were besieged by eager applicants for monk's orders.

Well for St Jude's Abbey at Ellington that the

The English Town

Abbot David was a level-headed man, and refused the hysterical, weak-kneed crowd who clamoured to become monks, and would have tired of the life as soon as the immediate danger was over. For many a monastery dates its decline from the Black Death, either because the monks shut themselves up in their abbey walls and left the sick and dying to themselves, or because they filled up their ranks with panic-stricken weaklings, who, as soon as they had recovered their senses, drank and diced and behaved in scandalous ways, to the lasting discredit of their monasteries.

The Black Death was followed by a series of troubled years. As has already been explained, the wars in France were going badly for England after 1360, draining away wealth and men from the land, and bringing in nothing, not even empty glories. That meant that Ellington, like other towns of England, went through years of trade depression, when the richest could but scrape a living, and the poor, but for the charity of the gild and of the monasteries, must have starved.

Meanwhile, the population of the town was increasing by leaps and bounds. For the Black Death had upset entirely the life of the countryside. In most parts of England by this time it had become the rule for the lord of the manor to accept a money payment in place of actual service, and

FOUNTAINS ABBEY

The chapel of Nine Altars, built by Abbot John of Kent in the thirteenth century.

From a drawing of 1843.

REAPING IN PLANTAGENET ENGLAND

The man with the staff and the horn is probably the reeve, the representative of the lord of the manor, whose duty it
was to make sure that the villeins paid their dues in labour and in kind.

From Queen Mary's Psalter, early fourteenth century.

that money payment was fixed and written down on the copies of the manor roll that each tenant held; but if the rent was fixed and could not be raised the price of labour was not. The Black Death left a great shortage of labour, a workman could demand double or treble his former wage, and get it, from lords anxious to get a little at least of their lands cultivated. Thus the lord received less rent than before, for many of the rent-payers were dead leaving no heirs to their holdings, and must pay more for the necessary labour to work their farms.

Naturally, the lords of the manors tried to overcome this disadvantage. Some demanded their old labour dues, since they could not hire men to work at reasonable rates. Others, and this was the usual plan around Ellington, took to sheep-farming. But the difficulty was that the ordinary manor was cut up into little patches of ploughed land, useless for pasturing sheep, and a lord could not turn off his tenants, so cunning lawyers were sought who put into force every possible irritating feudal right that the lord had possessed, but did not use. The result was to make the villein's life so irksome and unbearable that he ran away from his manor, which was just what the lord wanted, leaving the land free to be turned into sheep-grazing ground, where one shepherd could be employed instead of ten ploughmen, and more profit got from the sale of the wool than from the work of the ploughs.

Temporarily this brought great profit to Ellington, for the merchants of the town did a roaring trade in the wool from the manors around it. Also, dispossessed villeins wandered into the town, settled in houses and hovels left empty by the pest, and sought employment in unskilled labour, loading wool bales, general porter's work, and in the rougher trades as unskilled assistants.

Here was a new problem in English life, the problem of a class depending on labour entirely for their living, not possessing land or other property. And it was a class that tended to grow for two reasons : first, that there was an increasing demand for unskilled labour ; secondly, that freedom from the ties of landowning, when it meant that the holder was bound to his manor and must stay there, offered a certain attraction to adventurous and ambitious types. For a man who could move about could possibly discover a place where what he had to offer was badly wanted and would command a high price. Thus enterprising villeins would run away from their manors, make for a part of the country where labour was more than usually scarce, and become comparatively wealthy by hiring themselves out at huge wages.

From Sudden Death

But the unfortunate, lazy, and inefficient, among this class of landless labourers were indeed ill off. No longer had they the security of the manor, where except for deliberate rebellion a man could not be deprived of his patch of land and thus some sort of a living, nor did they belong to the town gilds. They depended upon casual charity, especially that of the monasteries, and created a problem for successive Governments that has lasted to this day.

The great nobles and landowners who ruled the land under the feeble Edward III in his disgraceful old age, when the warrior of Sluys and Creçy became a mere clod, tippling and snoring away his days in Westminster under the evil spell of Alice Perrers, and the same men ruling in the name of the boy Richard who succeeded the old King, had no doubt what to do. They simply passed through Parliament an Act which said that nobody should demand higher wages than were usual before the Black Death, that nobody should sell food at a greater price than before the Death, and that anybody found straying and refusing to work was to be branded and made a slave to the nearest landowner who wanted labour.

This might have solved the problem if anybody had obeyed the law, but nobody did, and, not having an efficient police force, the Government could not make them obey. As it was, it merely irritated everybody concerned, and made the Government very unpopular.

Then came the necessity for raising a tax to pay for the war in France, which England was steadily losing. Now in Edward III's reign a poll-tax had been tried—that is, a tax of so much for each person over sixteen in every village. This of Edward's had been graded, the rich had paid as much as five pounds, the poor as little as a penny or two apiece. But the process had been troublesome, and Richard II's regents tried another. A poll-tax was demanded of a shilling for each person, but it was proposed that in every district the authorities should arrange to collect more than a shilling from the wealthy, less from the poor. This was meant to have the same effect as the former tax with less trouble in collecting, but in fact it worked unfairly, for a poor district where there were no rich men would suffer, as every one would have to pay the shilling, while in a place actually better off the poorer sort would pay perhaps four or five pence each only, while half a dozen rich men paid four or five pounds each.

So the people of England set to work to defraud the Government, and I cannot better explain how than by telling the actual story of Ellington's scheme. When the numbers for the first poll-tax of 1379 were sent in there were found in Ellington:

300 married men
300 married women
 60 widows
 40 widowers
 80 boys over sixteen ⎫ unmarried
 99 girls   ⎭
———
879 Total

In 1381, when the second poll-tax was ordered, Ellington paid for:

240 married men
240 married women
 10 widows
  5 widowers
———
495 Total

There were apparently no unmarried men or women over sixteen, sixty married couples had died in two years, no new weddings had taken place, fifty widows, thirty-five widowers, all the unmarried folk of the town had vanished, for no known reason.

Of course nobody was deceived. There had been cheating on a huge scale to evade the tax. The town constable had been bribed or frightened into suppressing the existence of all who would not be able to pay the tax for themselves, such as unmarried children and old people whose families would have to pay, and had in addition been bribed to leave out of count whole families to cheat the tax-gatherers, for the method adopted was that the constable of each town or parish collected the tax and handed it over to travelling commissioners sent out by the King.

So the Government sent round commissioners again to make people pay the right amount of tax. These were set upon at a place called Brentwood in Essex, and when Chief Justice Belknap came to punish the rioters he too was beaten out of town and his clerks hanged. In Ellington the populace was less violent, they simply refused to pay another halfpenny, and in vulgar language told the King's commissioners that if they wanted more money they had better come and take it if they could. The commissioners wisely, for the sake of their own necks, decided that they couldn't, and went away with empty pouches.

But the smouldering fuel of rebellion, heated by the constant troubles and friction that I have described, was set ablaze by the mismanaged poll-tax. Wat Tyler, highway robber, old soldier, born general and leader of rebels, set Kent aflame. Jack Straw, John Grindcob, Richard Wraw, raised the Eastern counties. The people of places like St Albans and Bury St Edmunds rose in fury against the monasteries that owned the sites of their towns and had refused charters to the citizens. In London the mob cut the throats of Flemish weavers whom the London workers loathed and feared for their superior skill.

In Ellington there was a sudden rising of the poor unprivileged folk under one Tom the tinsmith, a rough, bearded giant with a gift for wild oratory. They were joined by rebel villeins from the country round, and together they burned the house of Master Timothy Stanwell, a lawyer of the town. He was unpopular with the villeins and workmen because of his employment by the local lords of the manor in their disputes with them, and with the townsfolk of the poorer sort because they regarded lawyers as dangerous allies of the master class. Rich burgesses were seized in the street and forced to cry: " God Save King Richard, and the Commons of England! "

Then came the Bishop of Norwich, riding north after Tyler had been killed in London and the pluck of the boy-king had broken the rebellion there. Tom the tinsmith was seized, and confessed his sins to the Bishop, who wore his robes above his armour. Then, having done his duty as a priest and absolved the rebel, the Bishop threw off his robes and had Tom and his chief lieutenants hanged and their heads stuck up over the lych-gate of the church. Law and order were restored

H

in Ellington, but the rebellion had left a terrible scar. Never again was there a feeling of trust and comradeship between rich and poor. The stupidity of the noble and middle class of England, unchecked by a strong king, had done irreparable damage to the social life of the country. Under a strong but greedy and unscrupulous monarch they were, as we shall see, to do yet worse evil.

CHAPTER IX

White Rose and Red

RICHARD II, the king with an ideal, had fallen before Henry of Lancaster, the business man, who paid in cash and privileges for his throne, and had no highfalutin schemes of governing the land for the good of all. There were two classes who might make themselves objectionable, the powerful noble and the wealthy merchant, and besides these was the Church, which suspected the dead King of sympathy with heretics, followers of Wyclif in England or Huss in Bohemia. " Very well," argued the canny Lancastrian, " I will keep these on my side, and the rest of the country can go hang." On these principles he proceeded to rule.

It is no part of our scheme, which deals with the town life of England, to show how this plausible plan went awry. Like many another before and after him, Henry IV and his successors found that class bribery simply encouraged those who received it to redouble their demands till at last, when they demanded so much that no

The English Town

Government could give it and remain a Government, there followed rebellion and civil war.

On the towns of England the coming of the Lancastrians had at first a good effect. Richard II had tried to stop the process of enclosure and check the development of sheep-farming, as he held that it brought more damage to the many than profit to the few. But under the Lancastrians sheep-farming went merrily on, and the towns that dealt in the wool that was now grown so lavishly all over the East and South of England grew and prospered.

The first symptom of that prosperity is a change in the nature of the chief institution of the town, the gild that ruled its trade and in most cases actually ruled the town as well.

Look again at the growing town of Ellington. When the charter was first granted to the town there were perhaps a score or two men of wealth and position trading within its boundaries. Now the score had grown to hundreds. New trades had sprung up in the land. There were weavers, shoemakers to produce those monstrous long-toed affairs beloved of the fifteenth century, goldsmiths and silversmiths, butchers, bakers, saddlers, ironmongers, cloth-mercers, tailors, and many another tradesman, dealing largely in goods that were not to any extent objects of trade in the days of Richard I, when domestic industry, each manor making what its own inhabitants required, was the general rule.

Now these things were made in towns and sold to country-dwellers, who sold their farm-produce in the town market to get the money to pay for what they needed.

Besides these common trades there were one or two very important and wealthy trades in Ellington, whose members were as exclusive and proud of their position as the knight on his manor in the country. There were the wool merchants, who bought up English wool, exported it to Antwerp and brought back thence mixed cargoes for sale in Ellington at fair-time. Then there were the shipwrights, a very skilled trade, mostly in the hands of two large families, the Wrights and the Dawkins.

Clearly, the one omnibus gild would not long accommodate so many and such diverse interests. There were furious quarrels among gildsmen of the different trades, especially between the wool brokers and shipwrights and their poorer brethren such as the butchers or shoemakers. Soon within the gild itself little cliques formed, grouped into trades. Nor were the only quarrels between rich and poor, aristocrat and commoner. There were troubles between trades whose interests overlapped. For example, it is probable that the age-long quarrel between butchers and leather-dressers goes back to this date. The butchers, of course, wanted to get as good prices as possible for the skins of the beasts they slaughtered. On the other hand, the leather-dressers wanted the skins cheap. The argument of each side went somehow like this.

Butcher: Why should I sell you my skins for next door to nothing when you will make a thumping profit out of the leather made from them?

Leather-dresser: Why should you make two profits from your trade where other folk only make one? Why should you make money first on the meat, then on the skins, above all, when those skins are but stinking offal till we have dressed and cured them and fashioned by our skill useful goods out of useless dross?

That was not the only quarrel, but it is typical. Clearly, the gild would break up under the strain. But the time for a town without gilds was not yet, so that what happened to the Gild of St Jude was what happens to a certain low type of animal when it breeds its young. The gild just split up into several gilds, one for each trade in the town. So that if we look at Ellington in the fifteenth century we shall find a score of craft gilds, instead of one merchant gild. But the government of the town still remains in the hands of the gilds. Freedom of the town can be gained only through membership of one or other of the craft gilds, and the inhabitant of the town who is not a member of any gild has no rights in the town, no voice in the choice of the mayor or aldermen, no means of bringing his grievances to the notice of the authorities, except by rioting and combining in unlawful assemblies to defy the town Government.

Now in Ellington, as in other towns, this class had been steadily growing for years. When trade was small and very restricted the tradesman needed no help beyond that of an apprentice or two who learned the trade while they helped their master. The apprentice must bind himself for seven years to obey his master, not to frequent ale-houses, gaming-houses, unlawful ' covens ' (that is meetings or assemblies), or to go off on his own amusement without that master's consent. In return for this the master must feed and clothe his apprentice and *teach him his trade*. Here, for instance, is Simon the shoemaker, stitching away at a pair of long shoes, while beside him Allan, his apprentice, works at the rougher, less skilled part of the task, but watches the clever stitches and neat rounding off of his master's work. Some day Allan will set up for himself as shoemaker, profiting by what he has learned under Simon's tuition.

But that idyllic state of affairs had gone by the fifteenth century. Even with the help of the gild it took some little capital to set up as a master, and those who did set up for themselves needed more assistance than their apprentices could provide. There came into being, therefore, the class known as journeymen—workmen, that is, who served a master for wages, not hoping to become masters themselves. And a pretty problem that provided for the town authorities.

Of course the idea of the nineteenth century, that a man was worth what wages he could get, was just as repugnant to the fifteenth century as the idea that a thing was worth what it would fetch in open market. The people of the fifteenth century tried to find both a just price, that is the exact price that gave the seller a fair profit for his risk and trouble, and a just wage, the exact wage that gave a man a fair return for his labour. Both these were repeatedly ordered to be fixed by the magistrates of every district, and varied if need be when conditions varied.

But the magistrates of Ellington were the mayor and aldermen, and, despite the fact that they were the chief employers of labour, no doubt they tried to be just. The task proved very difficult, for the price of food, despite every effort to fix it, would fluctuate up and down, according to local conditions, and a wage that was sufficient this year would be insufficient next. Also, as was only human, while the wage-earners accepted gratefully an increase in wages due to a bad harvest raising the price of food, they were much less ready to accept a reduction when a bumper harvest brought down the prices of corn. Besides all this, the machinery for fixing wages, periodical meetings and discussions by the magistrates was slow and cumbrous.

So the journeymen took to forming gilds of their own, which were promptly denounced as unlawful 'covens,' especially when they took to striking as a remedy for their grievances. One can sympathize with the authorities of Ellington and other towns of the period in their horror at this sort of thing. For a medieval town was ill-policed, and built mainly of wood, and a mob is a mob in all ages, liable to do senseless damage out of mere stupid temper. Supposing some heated agitator persuaded one of these riotous journeyman gilds to set fire to an unpopular master's shop, why, the whole town might be burned to the ground!

So when the first journeyman gild raised its head in Ellington it was suppressed with violence and its leader whipped out of town and branded for a dangerous rogue. But in secret these gilds continued to exist and stir up bad blood between master and man in the town. As always, the result was evil to the very men who hoped to benefit by these proceedings. For if the men united so would the masters, and against their workers; further, as long as masters were afraid of the possible results of the men's combination, the bad, harsh employer would have most influence on their councils.

The rich men, therefore, proceeded to establish their position by law, which, under the Lancastrians, was easy enough. For Richard II and the peasants of the revolt had agreed in one thing— both wanted a despotic monarch, and no privileged grades of society below him, all other men to be equal before the law. It was a rising of the privileged classes that had driven Richard from the throne, so of course Henry IV, their choice of monarch, could not object to these classes using Parliament to safeguard themselves, which they did by numerous Acts.

Hitherto the sending of members to Parliament had been looked upon as a grievance, for it cost money. Now that it was seen how Parliament could be used, people came to regard it as a privilege, and there was a good deal of competition for the honour of being a Parliament-man for your own shire or borough. But it is a mistake to imagine that the choice of the electors was free, or that the views of the House of Commons under the Lancastrians represented the views of the electors.

In Ellington, for example, the last of the Malin Earls of Ellington had immense influence, and the electors of Ellington would always choose the candidate recommended by him, provided he was not otherwise unsuitable. Earl Humphrey, on his part, always made arrangements with some suitable burgesses that they should have his patronage and support, provided they forwarded in the Commons the designs of the Earl and his friends among the great nobles who really ruled under this dynasty. As regards local affairs, the chosen candidate was left free to act as the interests of the town of Ellington required; so both parties were satisfied. The great nobles could use the Commons as a weapon to compel the King to their designs, the freeholders of the country and the gildsmen of the towns could use it to obtain such laws as would serve their local interests.

Wild was the cheering and great the enthusiasm of the good folk of Ellington when the news was brought of the great victory of Agincourt.

" Our English King Harry, God bless him," was the toast of the day, and good, easy burgesses met each other in the streets with wondrous tales of new successes in France—this town had fallen, that province submitted to the English King, and at last the very Crown of France had been surrendered to him by treaty, and then: " King Harry is dead; woe the day, the King is dead! "

It was true. The brilliant, selfish, short-sighted King was dead, leaving a legacy of war and disaster to his baby son, and a gang of uncles and cousins to rule the land. The Duke of Bedford, the only one among them of moderately decent character, was abroad in France. England was split into two factions, those who, like Humphrey of Gloucester and Richard, Duke of York, wanted to carry on the war with vigour, and, those who, like the Beaufort family and de la Pole, Earl of Suffolk, recognized the hopelessness of more fighting and wanted peace on good terms.

Meanwhile the hectic prosperity of the early Lancastrian period began to decline, for the boy-king could not keep order, the quarrelling regents would not. Every noble began to arm and badge retainers who would follow him even against the King, and small towns such as Ellington suffered. Pirates by sea, noble and ignoble robbers by land made trade insecure, and appeals to the King produced no effect. The townsfolk of England began to realize what fools they had been to ally with the nobles against the Crown, and when Richard of York, representative of the direct royal line, claimed the Crown the towns of England in the main favoured him.

" For," growled old John Writhesley, the Mayor of Ellington, " if York wins, look you, he is a strong man and no fool, and will rule this land as feeble Harry never could, no, nor dare to do, if he were twice the man he is. There will be peace then, and honest men can trade."

So through the struggles of the Wars of the Roses Ellington tended to favour York, the more so when the vigorous Queen Margaret of Anjou allied with the Scots and brought the wild men of the Northern counties marching down on London, who as they passed looted with extreme thoroughness the town of Ellington, held the Mayor to ransom, burned in sheer wantonness half the town, and generally made the name of Lancaster stink in the nostrils of the folk of Ellington.

Yet except for such sudden crises the life of Ellington went on very much as usual while the soldiers of York and Lancaster fought up and down the land. For the town, as a town, took no part in the battles, which were for the most part open fights between armies of hired partisans led by the nobility on either side, who, incidentally, changed sides with the persistence of so many Vicars of Bray. The armies fought and lost or won their battle, and then dispersed. They did not form regular bases on towns, so that siege warfare was unknown.

Thus, while a few of the poorer class in Ellington went off to join one army or the other, most stayed at home and did the best they could to secure a living by trade when neither roads nor sea were safe. True they had bursts of prosperity when, after a victory of York or Lancaster, the victors set out to dissipate the spoils in a mighty jollification ; for who could say when the other side would win, and what good is money to a dead man who cannot use it, or to a prisoner who if he keeps his head will be very fortunate and will certainly keep nothing else ?

Otherwise, trade was slack and depressed, and as usual the ill-paid classes suffered first, for naturally the struggling employer cut down his staff in time of stress. Therefore, all classes, except the turbulent feudal nobles, welcomed the coming of Edward IV, easygoing in his personal habits, but a stern ruler, fully aware of the value of trade to England, as he showed by his trade treaty with Flanders, and determined not to allow the rich nobles to rule in his name.

So the livery bands vanished from the land and pirates from the sea, and a brilliant if immoral Court created a demand for goods such as the merchants of England could supply. Peace brought prosperity, and in their prosperity the merchants of Ellington forgot the lessons of the Lancastrian period, that in the end strong rule is the best friend of trade, provided it is impartial strong rule, not biased to this or that class or interest.

CHAPTER X

Town Life at the End of the Middle Ages

WHEN the Wars of the Roses ended Merrie England was drawing near its close. Soon from cold Geneva under the snows was to come a religion that forbade merriment, and a time of change and struggle when serious ends and gloomy thoughts became natural to men who never knew from day to day what new crisis would be upon them. For the Wars of the Roses, fought though they were on English soil, had no such deep effects on the life of the people as had the rule of the Tudors, the Renaissance, and the Great Rebellion under Charles I.

Let us take a last look at Ellington of the Middle Ages, and consider the chain of events that began the transition to modern days and modern ways.

The keynote of the Middle Ages is stability. There are no such violent changes of fortune, or such differences between man and man as we find in later years. For a man to begin life with twopence in his pocket and end with a fortune was next door to impossible in those times. It would be hard to find a dozen men in Ellington with more than a thousand pounds in money and possessions, a great sum, but not to be compared with the fortunes of modern millionaires. On the other hand, the actual pauper was a rarity. There were plenty of poor, a few very rich, and a large number just comfortably off, but within reach of a monastery it was hard to starve, and the town authorities, too, did try to limit actual pauperism. Begging was quite a profitable trade, for charity was regarded as a Christian duty, though the frauds and violent rogues who took to begging as well as the genuine poor were making people more wary in their giving.

Yet the standard of comfort was still very low. Fireplaces with built-up chimneys were a new-fangled luxury. Feather-beds or even well-made hair mattresses were uncommon. The average man slept on a rough sack stuffed with straw, with another, or even a log of wood, for a pillow. Night-dresses were unknown, and baths a luxury of the very rich. If you were cold you slept in your ordinary day clothes, if it was hot, then naked. To have a separate sitting-room apart from the common dwelling-room and kitchen was a mark of wealth, and by the sturdy, old-fashioned burgess would be looked upon as ostentation.

Life, too, was very rough and harsh. The

punishments for the most trivial offences were brutal and severe. Here are a few from the records of Ellington:

John Palfrey, for stealing a horse, hanged.

Petronilla Witherstone, for throwing a stone at the Mayor and bruising his eye (what was her grievance, I wonder?), fifty lashes. The actual sentence was " to be stripped from the waist upwards and whipped through the town so that her back be all bloody."

Jasper Tulley, for heresy, declaring that a priest could not turn bread and wine into flesh and blood, imprisoned.

Jasper Tulley, for relapsing into heresy, burned alive. (In this case, evidently, the man had recanted and then after some time repeated his offence.)

William Feathers, robbery on the highway, escaped from justice, outlawed (*i.e.* might be killed at sight by anybody who met with him.)

Sarah Hughes, murdered her husband (petty treason), burned alive.

John Arkwright, high treason (concerned, apparently, in Scrope's rebellion against Henry IV), hanged, drawn, and quartered.

James Freeman (age twelve), stealing cloth to the value of five shillings, hanged.

The lot of the criminal was hard, though not as

hard as it became in later times under the Hano-
verians when the number of capital offences
mounted to ludicrous proportions. But the life of
the criminal was worth little as compared with the
safety of the community, and where police are non-
existent, or are inefficient, severity of punishment
is the natural attempt of the community to protect itself from the criminal.

Sickness, too, took dreadful toll of the lives of the
people. In Ellington we find that of every ten
children born six or more died before coming to
full age. Thus the population increased very little
in the country as a whole from the time of the
Black Death to the time of the Tudors, though
that of the towns tended to increase at the expense
of the country districts wherever sheep-farming
was the rule.

Dysentery, ague (a form of malarial fever), smallpox, sweating sickness, at intervals bubonic plague,
took dreadful toll of Ellington's population.
" This year was a pestilence of which died many
hundreds " is a common enough entry in the
records of Ellington town. Probably the doctors
killed as many as disease. Their medicines consisted of simple herbs and decoctions, which
probably did little harm, powerful, poisonous drugs
of mercury, gold, and arsenic solutions, which
undoubtedly did a great deal of harm, and magical

incantations, which may have done good by giving confidence to the patient.

But besides these they dealt in awful concoctions made of such matters as powdered human skulls, frogs' livers, crushed vipers, bulls' blood, powdered toad, and other horrors. One cure for the plague was apparently to split a living rat or cat in two and lay the bleeding, quivering corpse on the sore with the idea that thus the evil humours—that is, poisonous fluids which were supposed to be the cause of the pestilence—should be drawn out. Bleeding was applied for every ill, even battle wounds where loss of blood was already one of the patient's troubles, apparently because fever was regarded as a result of too much blood in the body. Simple amputations were, it seems, sometimes performed, but as a rule blood-poisoning carried off the victim.

On the whole only the strong and healthy had much chance of survival in the Middle Ages, though probably habit enabled the people to stand insanitary and hard conditions that would kill the modern easy-living Englishman, just as he would be killed by conditions under which the native of India not only lives, but thrives.

That is the dark side of the Middle Ages. Now to look at the lighter side.

The first noticeable thing is that there was

abundance of leisure. People who write to the papers to-day deploring the eagerness of the citizen to run off on holiday instead of sticking to his desk would have yet more cause to grumble had they lived in the Middle Ages. For then every saint's day, and there were a good number, was a public holiday, and rich and poor went out to enjoy themselves.

Now we talk a lot to-day about democracy. But the Middle Ages practised it. They did not believe that every one was, or could be, or indeed ought to be, equal. They did not allow 'the people' to rule themselves, they thought (were they wrong, I wonder?) that 'the people' would make a considerable hash of the business. But they did mingle in sport and worship, rich and poor together; there was not the tendency that exists to-day to carry class distinctions into church and into life. The truth is, of course, that there was less difference of habit and ideas between the various classes, especially once the rigid social grading of feudalism had broken down, than there is to-day. A rich man would not be revolted by the coarser habits of a poorer man, for his own habits were just as coarse. Both probably spat, swore, and ate noisily, and both spoke the local dialect, whatever it might be. The house of Alderman Howlet of Ellington and the house of

(*a*) A Wrestling Bout, to be followed by Cock-shooting

(*b*) Pig-sticking

From manuscripts of the early fourteenth century in the British Museum.

132

A TOURNAMENT IN THE EARLY FOURTEENTH CENTURY
From Queen Mary's Psalter, in the British Museum.

133

The End of the Middle Ages

John Walters the grave-digger were not so very unlike each other as the house of a rich merchant and a grave-digger of to-day would be. Their speech and personal cleanliness (or lack of it) were more or less the same. Their ideas of pleasure the same.

Chief among the pleasures of all ranks were the games and sports played in the common field or butts of the town. There was, of course, archery. This was practically compulsory, and every citizen was supposed to have a bow, and to know how to use it. It was looked upon as the duty of wealthy men to encourage this sport by offering substantial prizes for competitions, and it was a matter of some pride among the younger folk of the town to enter for these competitions. There were games not unlike football and tennis, not very popular with the authorities because they interfered with archery practice. Running and jumping were also much in favour.

Then there was dancing, especially on May Day and Midsummer Day, out in the open, a fine, enjoyable amusement. Tournaments, too, were to be seen among the nobles and gentry of the district, and no doubt the people flocked to them, and betted on their favourite knights as to-day on their favourite horses at Epsom. There was hunting, too, and hawking, for in many towns the freemen had the privilege of hunting small game and fowl on certain town lands, but this would be a more exclusive sport, confined to the richer folk.

Then there were the mystery plays. Every gild used to produce one of these once a year, usually at the summer festival of Corpus Christi. They were presented on raised stages wheeled through the streets, though at an earlier date they were given sometimes in the churchyard, or even in the church itself. They were meant to combine instruction with amusement, and were of two sorts.

The original mystery play represented some scene from the Bible, and is very interesting as showing the ideas on religion and public decency of our forefathers. It must be remembered that religion was of the very essence of their lives, yet they represented God Himself, or the Persons of the Trinity on the stage, which in these days would be regarded as blasphemous. But the organizer and writers of these mysteries, generally priests or clerks, thought nothing of doing this, or of bringing actors representing Adam and Eve on to the stage in white tights. They provided humorous relief too, to avoid boredom among their audiences, and the chief comic characters were Pontius Pilate, Judas Iscariot, and the Devil, who

134

are with us to-day disguised as Punch, Judy, and Toby. Withal, the religious feeling both of actors and audience was quite sincere, they saw nothing irreverent in all this, and, as most could not read, probably learnt quite a lot of religion from them.

The morality plays, which came later, showed various vices and virtues on the stage, each represented by an actor, and little plays were worked out, showing the consequences to Everyman of each sin or virtue. Here, too, comic relief was provided by an exhibition of slap-stick, cross-talk humour between Satan, Vice, and Virtue.

Such were some of the chief amusements of a town like Ellington, in addition to cock-fighting, bear-baiting, bull-baiting already mentioned, of which the last traces remain in the name bull-ring applied to a town square, and, of archery, such names as Newington Butts in London.

The government of the town has already been sketched, and that altered very little during the whole Middle Ages. There was a mayor and a body of aldermen chosen by the freemen of the town. Only the choosing body became more and more exclusive as years went by. At the beginning of the age of chartered towns such cases as that of Dick Whittington were not uncommon. There was plenty of scope for apprentices, plenty of demand for new men and new ideas, plenty of chances for an able man to rise if once he could get a footing in the gild, and that was not too difficult for a man who could pay his way. Of course the pantomime Whittington was almost an impossibility, but the real man, son of a Gloucestershire knight, who was apprenticed to a citizen, and rose to be Lord Mayor, was only one of many, and a late example at that.

But as the years went by the gilds grew more exclusive. The population of the towns began to increase, and there was no longer room for all comers. It became a difficult matter for one not the son of a freeman to become an apprentice in any town. Deliberately, in order to check migration from the country, the Government forbade agricultural workers to be admitted to gilds unless they were the children of substantial folk, and the gilds themselves tended to look with disfavour on outsiders and confine their membership to their own clique. So that while the number of inhabitants of the towns grew, the number of freemen did not, or at least not in proportion.

There could be no change in this as long as trade was local and petty. It is in the next age that trade expands, and then very curious things begin to happen to the town government, as we shall see. Yet with all their faults, and they had many, the gilds of England did a lot for our towns and deserve our gratitude. It is a thousand pities that they did not adapt themselves to changing conditions, and thus carry on their good work into a new and in some ways harder age.

But while the town looked after the amusements and punished the crimes of its inhabitants, the poor, the old, and the sick were not entirely neglected. There were town charities, generally the bequest of pious men for the benefit of their souls. One has already been mentioned, Ellington Grammar School. But there was also a hospital, a refuge for the aged and impotent, not as now a place for the treatment of the sick. This hospital, says the deed of foundation,

> shall be maintained for the care of such old, sick, and impotent persons as shall be from time to time named thereunto by the governors thereof [the mayor and three aldermen] so that the bedesmen of the hospital shall be men and women of good repute, not drunkards, idle, nor profane persons, and shall, if able to come and not let by sickness or impotence of age, duly attend Mass upon every Sunday and holy day, and shall if able to work perform such tasks suitable to their condition as the Governors shall allot to them.

Then there was Widow Bott's Charity. By this a piece of land outside the town was set aside, from the profits of which were to be provided each

year on the date of the foundress's death twelve
loaves and twelve sixpences, to be given to

> twelve poor widows of this town, being old and
> impotent, of godly life and sober conversation, the same
> to be chosen, and the dole distributed, by the clerk of
> the parish church of St Mary the Virgin for the time
> being.

Every gild too had its own private arrangements
for looking after sick poor folk. Yet despite this
there were beggars, people for whom there was no
room in the hospital, or whose moral character did
not qualify them for its benefits. These would
often add robbery, fortune-telling, or cheating to
their other avocations, and will be more fully
described in the chapter on the vagrancy problem.
They gave the town authorities a great deal of
trouble, and no really satisfactory scheme was
worked out for dealing with them till Elizabeth's
reign.

Such was the life of a town during the closing
years of the Middle Ages. We must consider now
what changes took place when the events that
begin the Modern Age occurred.

CHAPTER XI
A New World

TO understand the change that came over English town life during the two centuries, say, 1450 to 1650 we have got to understand a little about the Renaissance—above all why it should have taken place at all.

The Middle Ages were, as I have said, ages of stability. They were also inclined to be ages of stagnation. It is amazing how much smaller is the difference between the mental equipment of a man of 1050 and a man of 1350, than between the latter and a man of 1550. The reason is that a great change had taken place in the circumstances of the world between these last two dates.

Now the Renaissance was originally nothing but the rediscovery of certain facts and ideas known to the ancient world, and forgotten or half forgotten during the Middle Ages. What followed, the spate of new discoveries and adventures, was the natural result of the Renaissance, but it was not itself the Renaissance.

To understand that we have to consider the first spreading of Christianity. When Christianity began to get a hold on the Roman world Rome. was already on the downward path. The religion of Jupiter and the gods had degenerated into a mass of stupid and ugly superstitions, mixed with all sorts of weird Oriental religions introduced from Egypt and other conquered lands of the Empire. The other great race of antiquity, the Greeks, were at the bottom of the hill down which the Romans were tumbling. They were degenerate and effeminate, composing pretty-pretty love-songs for the Roman masters. There were learned men in Greece and Rome, but those learned men were tainted with the vile habits of their age, when manhood and decency seemed lost for ever.

Then came the Barbarians, good healthy savages from the North-east, who cleaned up the rotten old city of Rome. But they failed to sweep away Christianity, which in course of time established itself as the religion of the new rulers of Europe as it was of the old.

Now a good many of the decadent learned men of Rome had vanished in the great spring-cleaning of the Barbarian invasion, and the new men, fierce-hearted fighting men, who had, moreover, to defend the new lands they had conquered from other invasions out of the teeming East, had little time for learning. Only the clergy of the Christian

Church, secluded from all this in their strong-walled monasteries, were able to learn and write books. Thus the work of educating others fell into their hands.

But the clergy were Christians first, learned men second. They approved heartily of such knowledge as would help a man to get to Heaven, other knowledge they regarded as useless, possibly harmful. Especially did they regard classical learning as dangerous, and that for a good reason. The conquest of Europe by Christianity was no easy matter, there were always people eager to go back to the older religions; probably the witches, who certainly existed, though most of the legends about them are false, were such people, secret worshippers of older gods. Thus all through the Middle Ages learning was strictly censored by the Church, and as a rule only Churchmen were learned at all. Ordinary folk had quite enough to do, fighting and tilling the soil, and had no time to learn. And, as the clergy were interested in the next world rather than this, many ideas and pieces of knowledge familiar to the ancient world were simply forgotten in the West.

Then came days when men who were not clergy began to have more leisure, and to look round the world. And they found that the clergy, who could read and write, had secured all the high offices of state, such as chancellor and judge, and so on. But, with leisure, ordinary laymen began to seek such posts, and demand education so that they could get them, and the education that they needed was very different from that needed for a priest. These were interested in holy things, the layman in making a good living on this earth. The friars, probably out of sheer opposition to the monks, proved willing to supply a more general education, and it is probably to them that we owe much of the growth of Oxford and Cambridge Universities that took place during the thirteenth century.

That was the beginning of the Renaissance, for many men who had begun to learn found the process fascinating, and went on for the sake of finding out things.

Something lost beyond the ranges . . .

That line of Kipling's applies to such men as Roger Bacon or Humphrey, Duke of Gloucester. Something was lost beyond the dark hills of ignorance, and they set out armed with strange books and stranger instruments to find it.

That was the beginning of the Renaissance, but at first it languished for lack of material. Then came the taking of Constantinople by the Turks, and the Greek scholars, who had lived in safety behind the massive walls of Byzantium, as the place was then called, must fly for their lives, taking their precious manuscripts with them.

Here was learning that the Church had either forbidden or taught in mutilated form. The arguments of Aristotle, the theorems of Euclid, the engineering speculations of Archimedes, all could be learned from these refugees from the conquered city. Men began to think for themselves instead of accepting whatever they were told. The Renaissance was in full swing. Then came the invention of printing, and a hundred might read what before was confined to the few.

That was the Renaissance. Its results were incalculable, but the first that affected the position of the English town was undoubtedly the discovery of America. This was a direct consequence of the Renaissance, that enabled a rough sea-captain of Genoa to learn that certain ancient authorities had believed the world was round, and sent him sailing westward to reach India and far Cathay, countries that could otherwise be reached only by a long overland journey, or perhaps by rounding the Cape of Good Hope.

That discovery was the beginning of the decline of Ellington and, indeed, of a large number of England's older towns. For it transferred the centre of the English shipping trade from the

The English Town

East Coast to the West, and diminished the importance of the wool trade now that trade with new lands became possible. Venice ceased to be the chief trading town of Europe, sending its treasures overland to Flanders, and the primacy of trade was transferred to Spanish and Portuguese cities, whence, as far as England was concerned, it was easier to bring goods to Falmouth or Bristol or Southampton than to the old port towns of the East Coast.

But this decline was not immediate. For the moment the Renaissance, with its spirit of search and adventure, gave new life to English trade everywhere. It also changed the face of the English town, for men began to build either private houses or public buildings according to the principles of Greek and Roman architecture, modified to suit English weather and English ways. Something more elaborate, more highly decorated, and more pleasing to the eye than the simple barn-like hall began to rise in country and town alike. The parish church ceased to be the only outstanding piece of architecture in many a small town about this period. The climax of Renaissance ideas in building is to be seen in the St Paul's Cathedral that Christopher Wren built when the older structure perished in the Great Fire.

Manners too began to soften, first among the

CHICHESTER MARKET CROSS

Erected in 1500 by Bishop Story, at the point where the intersecting Roman roads of the
ancient town of Cissæ Castrum met. — The market cross was a characteristic feature
of the medieval town or village. There wandering preachers held forth, there farmers
and merchants foregathered, bargains were concluded, and royal proclamations were
made.

144

OLD HOUSES AT RYE
Photo F. Frith and Co., Ltd.

A New World

higher classes, who, as they travelled abroad a good deal—another symptom of the new age—had more chance of seeing and adopting new ideas. Comfort, such as nightdresses and feather-beds, began to be regarded. The art of living was now as important as the art of living a religious life had been in the Middle Ages.

Music, poetry, fine writing, and painting, things that had been for the few, and especially the clerics in the Middle Ages, were now honoured by every man who claimed to be a man of culture.

But the moral effects were not so good. For the Renaissance led to the questioning of accepted teachings of the Church as well as of accepted ideas on other matters. And among the most important teachings of the medieval Church was this, that a man who had wealth or power or position was responsible to God for the use that he made of his gifts. Now, with a wave of disbelief in the teachings of the Church, this idea too began to decline. " Get what you can, spend it on yourself, for who knows whether there is any God ? " was the general feeling of the day, and even the coming of the Puritan did not mend matters, for he was so occupied with his numerous duties toward God that he forgot too often his duty toward his neighbour that Our Lord gave as the second of His great commandments.

K

The English Town

We see this clearly enough in the life of Ellington at this period. Rich merchants begin to grow yet more wealthy, but at the same time the genuine pauper, the man who wants work and cannot get it, begins to appear in some strength. The feeling in the town between rich and poor grows more bitter, charity less common and less spontaneous.

We can see the beginning of a new age in the attempt of Will Stukely, a clothier of Ellington, to found what we should now call a factory. He hired a large barn, fitted it with looms, bought a great amount of raw wool, and engaged men to make up the wool under his own supervision. This is what is called the capitalist system, and it has great advantages over the old system by which one man bought his raw material, made it up, and sold the finished article in his own little shop. It would be best to leave till we come to the Industrial Revolution the discussion of its exact advantages over the old system. But it must be said at once that for the capitalist system to succeed the employer, who provides the capital and pays the wages, *must* realize his responsibilities toward those he employs. The vice of the capitalist from the Renaissance period till quite lately has been his refusal to do this.

The Government, it is true, did try to check the unpleasant developments from these new ideas, but the cynical, sordid Tudor rulers, and that most sordid of all, " Good Queen Bess," did little to prevent the newly enriched man using his wealth as he liked, for on that class to a great extent they depended for the throne to which the illegitimate descendants of John of Gaunt had little other claim. When a more honest race, the Stuarts, came to the throne the rising tide of industrial selfishness proved too strong for them, and was partly responsible for sweeping away the House of Stuart into exile and poverty.

To revert to Will Stukely, his attempt to start the factory system was a failure, for the gilds, who disliked anything of the sort, drove him out of business. But the attempt is a sign of the times. The Renaissance rang the death-knell of the gilds as the controlling force in town life. For this the gilds are themselves partly to blame. They were set in certain ways, and would not budge from them. They opposed anything new just because it was new, not distinguishing between good and bad, but lumping all alike in one sweeping hatred. The consequence was that while many hated the gilds merely because the gilds did insist on a certain standard of fair play in trade relations, others opposed them because the gilds would not allow a progressive and efficient man to use his skill to the best advantage, even though he might be prepared to submit to some regulation of his activities in the interests of the country in general.

The combination of these two groups destroyed the gilds, and to this day nothing has been found to take their place. But had the gilds welcomed the progressive manufacturer and assisted him, instead of opposing him out of sheer prejudice, they might have survived, for on the matter of fair trade both the Government, if they had dared to put their thoughts into practice, and public opinion were with the gilds. But there was a growing demand for novelties that the gilds would not supply, and for cheap, quickly made stuffs that, under the gild system, could not be supplied, and in consequence the gild declined, while the independent manufacturer throve. Unfortunately, if the independent manufacturer was a heartless rogue, there was no organization to stop him oppressing his poorer neighbours at will, except the Star Chamber, which was, in consequence, loathed by the merchants of the new age, and abolished as soon as they had sufficient power.

Such was the new England that followed the Renaissance. There was more luxury, more refinement; even the poorer classes shared in the general rise of the standard of life. But several problems were raised which in all the years from that day to this we have failed to solve. The number of paupers was increased, and the old safeguards which had made destitution next door to impossible were broken down because they made very difficult the gaining of immense wealth, with which could be secured the luxuries, mental and material, that the Renaissance made available.

The Renaissance, too, weakened the position of the one power that might have taken the place of the gild as the arbiter of fairness between man and man, that of the Crown. The records of Greece and Rome were distinctly republican in their ideals, and men began to dream of something like the Roman Republic, in which the wealthier classes ruled the rest for their own advantage, forgetting the end of that story, which was that from the wealthier classes power passed to the common people, and from them to a despotic Emperor as the only alternative to anarchy and ruin brought on by the bitter struggles between class and class.

The stage was set for a new act. Enter Henry Tudor—the eighth English king to bear that name—selfish, overbearing, gross in body and mind, and the tragedy began.

CHAPTER XII

The Reformation and the Vagrants

NEWS of the King's act in cutting England off from the Church at Rome was received with mingled feelings in the prosperous wool-trading town of Ellington.

There were those who applauded the action. The upper class in and about the town had long been jealous of the wealth and influence of the Church, and the merchants, who desired national prosperity above all things, disliked the interference of the Church in English affairs. With some, too, there was a genuine feeling that religion ought to be reformed in England. There were those who had studied the groundwork of religion in the light of the new learning and felt that the Church did not practise what it preached. There were others whose approval of the King's action was merely sordid and grounded on the basest of motives. These were the get-rich-quick party in the town, who chafed under the restrictions that the Church imposed upon trade. It must, however, be admitted that the Church, like the gilds, stuck to reasonable and unreasonable restrictions alike. There was plenty to be said for the Church's objection to practices such as forestalling, that is, cornering the market in necessaries of life and forcing up their prices. There was nothing to be said for the Church's objection to a man who had not enough money for an enterprise borrowing what he needed at a reasonable rate of interest.

On the other hand, the poor folk of the town were horrified. To them the Church was the Holy Mother; they looked with superstitious but genuine reverence on its ceremonies and rules. It provided them with something to live for in this world and the next.

But when the next act in the awful drama was staged opinion in Ellington was far more united against the Crown. For there came one day three men who subjected the abbot and monks of St Jude's Abbey to a rigorous cross-examination, and went away bearing evil report of their lives.

Now this the people of Ellington knew to be false. True, the abbot and his monks were easy-going folk, not noticeably much more religious than those about them, and there had been occasional grumbles at their slackness, but they were kindly landlords, decent neighbours, harmless, if sometimes a little slow and disinclined to join in the hustle of changing affairs. They were charitable too, giving shelter to the homeless, comfort to the sorrowful, and attention to the sick. Even Father Gilbert, the parish priest of Ellington, and he had had his quarrels with the monks at times, spoke in their favour.

But the King was determined and encouraged in his determination by such men as the Seymours and Dudleys, men of middling fortune who meant to become, by hook or by crook, great and wealthy nobles. The Malins had gone, killed out in the Wars of the Roses, and the new Earl of Ellington, John Stamner, a man of lowly ancestry, licked his lips as he thought of the fat lands of the abbey that he meant to add to his own estate. So out into the world the monks had to trudge, and the abbey, roofless, for the lead of the roof was worth money, despoiled of its treasures, desolate, stood there empty, a quarry for successive generations of builders, till to-day but a few grassy ruins tell us where once it stood.

That brought Robert Aske and his men marching down from Lincolnshire and Yorkshire, and with one accord the poorer and middle sort of the men of Ellington rallied to his standard. The new Earl must skulk in his castle, for nowhere else was he safe, and those of the burgesses of Ellington who approved the dissolution of the monasteries found it wisest to keep their opinions to themselves.

The rising failed, however. The cunning of the

The Reformation and the Vagrants

Tudor, and the solid support of the new nobility and the moneyed men of London and the South proved too much for Aske's hastily organized army. There were rotting heads above the gate of Earl Stamner's castle, and the people of Ellington submitted because they must.

Then, like a flood, the vagrancy problem was upon them. It had been masked hitherto by the charity of the monasteries. Now the homeless wanderer had no place to lay his head. He must beg, steal, or starve.

The problem itself was not new. Ever since the Black Death there had wandered about England idle men of a criminal type, who lived by their wits. They varied from merry rogues like Shakespeare's Autolycus—

> The white sheet bleaching on the hedge . . .
> Doth set my pugging tooth on edge—

to dangerous gangs who would hold up a town to ransom if they were strong enough, or commit every species of mischief within its boundaries if they were not, defying the few town constables to deal with them, driving the magistrates to despair.

Let us look at a typical gang who came to Ellington once at fair-time, and kept the town in a panic for three whole days, till at last the citizens organized themselves into a body and drove them out.

The English Town

Their leader was called the 'Upright Man,' a rascal with the brains of a clever officer, able to organize and control a motley gang of rogues as bad or worse than himself. A tall fellow, with a wicked, scarred face and straggling beard, he had seen service in Europe, and wandered back from the wars a dangerous man, disinclined for regular work, yet determined to make a good living.

Then there was Bartholomew and his party, 'mumpers' as they were called, who feigned disease or lameness, and 'mumped,' that is, begged, in a peculiar, whining sing-song that anyone can hear to this day who goes to Eastern lands where this sort of beggar is still common. But if they came upon a lonely household, especially if the man of the house were absent, then the lame walked, and the blind saw, and the diseased became suddenly hale and hearty, beat the wretched housewife to death, or at best locked her and her children into an empty room, and took whatever they desired.

There were Abraham-men too in the gang who shammed mad and asked for charity, like the 'mumpers,' taking it by force if they dared. Then came the coney-catchers, swindlers, players with cogged dice, confidence-trick men.

Such were the vagrant gangs who were so dangerous to the peace of England in the days of the

154

The Reformation and the Vagrants

Tudors. They were not a new problem, but the sudden growth of enclosure for sheep-farming, which the Tudors would not check (because they depended on the support of the new nobility who took this method of making quick profits), led to the eventual damage of the towns of England as will be seen, and the dissolution of the monasteries, added to the numbers of these gangs, and made them sullen and desperate. They were more ready to take to crime now that the monasteries no longer stood open to give them a night's rest and food.

Besides these criminal gangs there were many solitary vagrants, dispossessed farm-labourers, expelled monks, and others, wandering from place to place in search of work, begging as they wandered.

The problem that confronted Ellington was terrible in its extent and difficulty, for there was no organization to deal with such a case as this. The gild charities were for their own members, and in any case the wealth of the gilds was beginning to decline. Town charities were strictly limited, and the revenue of the town was small.

Moreover, the city fathers of Ellington were not in charitable mood. They were new men, eager, hard-headed men of business, who did not trouble to regard the difference between the genuine out-of-work and the criminal fraud. Besides, they had their own unemployment problem in Ellington itself, for the merry Tudor monarch, unsatisfied with the wealth of the monasteries, had debased the coinage, and thus brought bad times upon such towns as Ellington, already past their prime.

So the matter was brought up in Parliament, and we may be sure that the two burgesses returned for Ellington pressed hard for some suitable law. They got it.

Every person wandering without means of subsistence was to be whipped and sent back to his or her parish—if caught again to be branded, and the third time to be hanged.

But even the hard-hearted Tudor Justice of the Peace was not prepared to apply this law in all its severity, especially in the country, where old-fashioned country landowners were at the head of local government. And when one or two of the sterner justices of Ellington tried to apply the law they found that the difficulty was that they could not discover to which parish they must send the whipped vagrant, so just had to let him loose to be whipped again somewhere else. Also, a number of wanderers from Ellington returned compulsorily to their home parish, and there was no method of dealing with them.

So the law remained chaotic, enforced with severity in some places, not enforced at all in others, and the vagrants, suffering under a sense of injustice—for who could feel that it was right to be punished merely for being poor?—became desperate and yet more dangerous.

It was not till Elizabeth's reign that the problem was in part solved, when a rate was collected in each parish to set the genuine vagrant to work, and the fierce punishments of whipping, branding, and hanging were applied only to " sturdy rogues and vagabonds "—*i.e.*, determined criminals of the vagrant class who would not work when work was offered.

But the people of Ellington soon had other things to think of than the vagrants. For when the consumptive young prig, Edward VI, came to the throne, his Regents, first Seymour and then Dudley, set to work to complete the spoliation of religion begun by Henry VIII. First the lovely carvings and rich jewels of the parish church were summarily taken away. There was grumbling in the alehouses, and treason spoken in the streets, but the rulers of England were too strong to be upset. The only result of grumbling was swift and severe punishment.

Then came the preachers of a new faith, gloomy, fierce fanatics, who hated the games and amusements of the common people, and would have abolished the maypole and saints' days and all the happy, natural sports of the land. But they were welcomed with open arms by the new men among the merchants. Their gloomy creed suited the hard materialism of the new-rich. Above all it combined the advantages of both worlds, or could be made to do so by an easy bit of hypocrisy.

For the Catholic faith had put great reliance on good works, hence the doctrine of indulgences, that allowed the ordinary sinner the benefit of the good deeds and prayers of the saints. This had been scandalously abused by certain Popes, and in protest the extreme Protestants denied that good works, that is living a good life and doing good deeds, were any use at all. Only by faith, by being one of God's chosen, could a man be saved. A very natural reaction from the other doctrine!

But, and this was its danger, it attracted such men as William Horler, a clothier of Ellington town, whose speciality was making cheap and shoddy clothes, paying his labourers starvation wages, and misrepresenting the quality of his goods, venial sins according to the new view of commercial morality that was beginning to prevail, but regarded as serious crimes by the old Church. Yet Horler was a superstitious man, and feared hell fire. Here was a religion that promised him heaven if only he accepted certain rather savage beliefs, went to church to hear long sermons on Sundays, and avoided games and sports which this new creed regarded as wicked, and he regarded as waste of time and money. Also, as this new religion frowned upon saints' days as superstitious, he could get more work done in the week than under the old arrangements for the same pay.

It would be grossly unfair to suggest that this Horler was a typical Puritan, but it is idle to deny that there were such men, and their number tended to increase as commerce became more and more hard-headed and individual, and commercial men more and more inclined to resent dictation as to their methods of trading, yet not inclined to deny religion altogether—a rare attitude as yet. Besides this, these rich commercial men could and did dictate the general policy of Puritanism when it became a political force, and are responsible for the reputation for long-faced hypocrisy that still clings round the name of Puritan.

These men it was who encouraged Edward VI's Government in their next act, the confiscation of the funds of the gilds because, so they said, a great deal of the gilds' money was devoted to superstitious purposes—prayers for the souls of dead gild brethren who had left money to their gilds on that condition. The confiscation of the chantries too, little chapels founded with the same object, brought hardship to large parishes such as Ellington, for the chantry priests had acted as curates for the overdriven parish priest. Now Ellington must go without their services.

The confiscation of the gild funds was far more serious. For the hospital went, that charity that had provided for the old and sick, because one of the clauses in the deed of foundation required the bedes-folk to pray for the founder's soul. Widow Bott's Charity of loaves and sixpences went the same way, into the greedy pockets of King Edward's courtiers. Only the Grammar School escaped, but narrowly, and that owing to the protests of Archbishop Cranmer, the one comparatively honest man among the crew of rogues who ruled in the name of the boy-king.

For the time being this meant ruin to the town of Ellington. No longer could the gilds keep up either their work or their charities, they became mere empty shells, forms persisting void of life or intelligence. It was still necessary to be a member of a gild to be a freeman of the town, but this only gave a small group of rich men who remained in the town the opportunity to restrict the town government to themselves and their friends. Old towns began to decline, new towns, where there were no gilds, to rise. It is from this period that the Black Country of the Midlands begins to grow, though only slowly as long as wood charcoal is used to smelt iron. But the beginnings of Birmingham and other similar towns are to be found in the migration to them of independent merchants from old gild towns, first because they disliked the restriction of the gilds, and then because of the ruin that too often followed the confiscation of gild funds.

It was the fishing trade and some remnants of the wool trade that tided Ellington over these evil days, to sleep for some time, waking again when certain new developments brought fresh life to the town. But never again was the wool trade the staple trade of England. Greed had brought its own reward. Men who had depopulated acres of fine arable country to grow rich quickly on sheep-farming suddenly found that the bottom had fallen out of the wool market, for the perfectly simple reason that they had produced too much wool, and lowered the price to such a degree that sheep-farming ceased to be profitable.

The Age of Manufactures was now about to begin, after a time of struggle and conflict, in which the religious and political aspects have too often blinded us to the social conflict that was proceeding at the same time. It is with this that the next chapter deals.

CHAPTER XIII
New against Old

THE Age of Elizabeth really opened the New World to England, a world hitherto the preserve of Spain and Portugal. It is an amazing period. At home reigns a woman, with the brain and will-power of a strong man, determined to make her country great, yet at the same time grasping and cynical in character, aided by two great Ministers: Burleigh, narrow, honest, and painstaking; Walsingham, a sly, precise Puritan, who thinks no action vile that contributes to his main object, the overthrow of Spain. Under this curious Government England begins to forge ahead and prosper. Nor was this solely an age of gross material gain. There was far too much of that spirit in it, but it gave us as well Sidney, Ben Jonson, and Shakespeare.

For Ellington town Elizabeth's Age was a period of temporary revival of prosperity. The great centre of trade and commerce was still in the South-east, only very slowly did it move to the Midlands, and Elizabeth, whatever her bad qualities, was at least financially honest. She restored a sound coinage, and secured peace and order throughout the land, the two prime necessities of trade. Shipbuilding and fishing flourished, and a new trade began to grow to great proportions, the weaving of woollen cloths.

This had been the staple trade of Flanders, and throughout the Middle Ages English weaving had been regarded as crude and coarse. But when the Netherlands revolted against Philip of Spain a great many skilled weavers from that country made their way to England, and settled down, as did a good many French Huguenots who were also skilful craftsmen. So again the streets of Ellington were filled with bustling feet, the houses with the whirr of looms.

The essential trouble that was to break out in the next reign was, however, there, under the fair-seeming surface of life. That trouble was not, as certain people like to state, that the capitalist system was taking the place of the older domestic system, for that was a natural and inevitable process; the old domestic gild system simply could not cope with a trade that was growing every day to meet the needs of a growing population and foreign trade as well. What was wrong was the type of capitalist who came to the fore, and that was due in a great degree to the loosening of the bonds of morality and public

163

decency that followed the disgraceful Reformation of Henry VIII.

It is not here the place to decide on the necessity for some sort of Reformation, but it can hardly be denied that Henry VIII was actuated by mere greed and ambition in his attack on the Church of Rome, and that being so, he had to foster and secure the help of men as greedy and unscrupulous as himself. Professor Bain [1] considers that this is the main source of our difficulties from Henry's day to this, and there is something to be said for the view. It is certain that the capitalist system, set going during a period of open greed and plunder, started on wrong lines, and is only now beginning to find where its true interests lie.

There were, no doubt, good and generous employers, but they would find it hard to compete with unscrupulous men who could undersell them owing to the low wages they paid and their questionable methods. That that was the case we can see by looking at the Statute of Apprentices. For by that law manufacturers are forbidden to take on more than a certain number of apprentices, unless they employ a certain number of workmen; evidently men had been making money by using apprentices (who were of course unpaid, as assistants. This was manifestly unfair, for the

[1] *History of English Monarchy.*

master covenanted to teach his apprentice his trade, which he clearly could not do if he employed him as an ordinary workman, and it gave the man who did so an unfair advantage over honest traders who paid for their labour. The practice must have been fairly common to need a special law against it.

The trouble was that Elizabeth depended very largely on the trading class for her throne, and therefore dared not anger them by strictly enforcing this law, and, as we shall see, the result was trouble, when, under the Stuarts, the law *was* put into force, together with many other laws meant to protect the workman and the country in general against the greed of individual manufacturers. As it was, trouble was only postponed by the pressing danger from Spain.

Meanwhile, amid alarms and excursions, changes of immense importance were taking place in Ellington and towns like it. The streets were beginning to assume a more modern form, better and bigger houses were being built, and there were even people who talked about some elementary form of sanitation, but they were laughed at by the ordinary folk. Brick was beginning to take the place of timber and mud, and the Queen's Council, through the Star Chamber, encouraged every scheme of town planning that was brought forward, which did not endear the Star Chamber to the merchant class, for the Government's ideas were expensive and troublesome. The Star Chamber was the king's own special Court, that could and did enforce the king's will on the magistrates and rulers of the counties and cities of England.

For instance, on a petition from certain inhabitants of Ellington a certain Master Godling was forbidden to turn out a number of people from a crowded part of the town in order to build himself a mansion. " Star Chamber oppression," yelled Godling and his friends, yet it is not surprising that among the poorer people of England the terrible Star Chamber was by no means unpopular, for in the country too the Star Chamber did what it could, which was not much, to regulate enclosures so that the poor should not suffer too greatly in the process, insisting that when enclosure took place land should still be kept under the plough, and inhabited cottages should not be destroyed.

The difficulty, of course, was that these orders must be enforced by the local Justices of the Peace, often the offenders themselves, or their friends, and that even the Star Chamber could not control powerful courtiers, so that their schemes did not work very well, especially under Elizabeth, who had a horror of making herself unpopular. Thus the Star Chamber got itself hated, without very

THE GUILDHALL AT EXETER

This is probably the oldest municipal building in England. The rear part was rebuilt in 1464; the front was erected in 1593.

Photo F. Frith and Co., Ltd.

166

THE VILLAGE OF LAVENHAM, SUFFOLK

On the left of the picture is the fourteenth-century Wool Hall, the home of a cloth gild when cloth was an important village industry. The present building has been carefully restored. For three centuries Lavenham was famous for its

much benefit to the country. That in another two hundred years the Star Chamber might have become a very efficient local government board is probable enough, but it was never to have a chance.

Meanwhile Puritanism was increasing steadily in Ellington town. Cartwright and his friends at Cambridge had introduced into England the full-blown doctrine of Presbyterianism, and it was popular with the merchant class for several reasons.

In the first place, most of the country squires and nobles were Churchmen, and enmity between town and country was beginning to grow, for in many respects their interests differed. But we shall find that during this period, all over Europe, political or social feuds generally took on the colour of religion. For example, the nobles of South France disliked the policy of the French kings, who were trying to bring all France under strong central rule. They rebelled, but they said that they were rebelling for religion. In the same way the Scottish nobles, who disliked the policy of the Catholic Mary of Guise, the Regent of Scotland, promptly turned Presbyterian. Thus, when there was dislike and distrust between the merchant class and the older type of landowner, who was either Church of England or Catholic, the merchant took up Presbyterianism.

The English Town

Then, again, the refugees from the Netherlands and France were Presbyterian in their religion, and thus it spread to those among whom they settled. Besides which, as has already been explained, Presbyterianism, though it interfered with a man's amusements and private life, left him very free on matters of commercial morality, and so attracted the merchant. Not that the sincere Presbyterian would have allowed any such thing, but there can be little doubt that the merchant found the religion of Calvin less inclined to cavil at hard bargaining or low wages, as long as there was no open cheating, than that of the Church of England, especially when, under Whitgift and Laud, the High Church party, who agreed with the Catholic Church on these matters, came to the fore.

Lastly, Presbyterianism was a republican religion, governed by elected groups, ' synods ' they were called, and the merchant class was attracted by the example of Venice, a commercial republic where the merchant ruled. In England power was in the hands of the Crown and the country gentlemen, who were not too favourable to the demands of the merchant class. The Stuarts especially considered that the money-making interests of the trader and manufacturer should give way to the interests of the country in general. Should Presbyterianism get a foothold in England it would undoubtedly enable the merchant to control the Crown through religion, and thus in political matters as well.

Till the Armada was defeated, however, nothing much happened. In Ellington a few Puritans who became too noisy were punished by the Star Chamber. One man, for instance, had his hand cut off for publicly burning Elizabeth's prayer-book, which he called a " foul Popish Mass-book full of vain fables." Another was pilloried for crying out against the proposed marriage of the Queen and a French Prince as a plot to bring Popery into England. But as the alternative to Queen Elizabeth was Mary, Queen of Scots, the Presbyterian merchants of Ellington, though they grumbled, did no more.

When James Stuart came to the throne matters were very different. The Spanish danger was over, no longer was there the peril that England might fall beneath the heel of Spain. James, in fact, was inclined to friendship with Spain, and the merchants of England were furiously hostile.

" There can be no peace with Rome and Satan," cried one enraged shipowner of Ellington to another when news of the proposed treaty was brought to the town.

" Aye," snarled another, " peace with Spain forsooth, and I just ready to sell a new-built ship to Sir Walter Raleigh for an expedition to the Indies."

"And I," chimed another, "have lent one hundred good pounds to Master Tom Longstaffe, who proposes to seize a galleon or two upon the Main. Why, 'twill be ruin, I say, if peace is made."

Then a new grievance arose. James put into force the laws of Elizabeth, and merchants who employed too many apprentices, engaged men for short periods and then turned them off to do as best they might, sold inferior goods, and other offenders of this class were suddenly and roundly fined by the Star Chamber.

Then came monopolies. For example, James I wanted to found a soap industry in England in order to create employment. He therefore gave a monopoly in the manufacture of soap to a London company. The shippers of Ellington and the other port towns of England were furious; they made a good deal of money by importing soap, and a petition was got up signed by merchants from all over England alleging that the monopoly soap was bad. Judge of their rage when the Council actually had the soap tested, and found it to be as good as the imported French article.

Hence the bitter opposition of the town members of Parliament to the Stuarts, and the towns were grossly over-represented. For of some 400 members of Parliament at least 300 were borough members, but the proportion of town-dwellers to country-dwellers was certainly not three to one, indeed it is doubtful if the total town population of England at this period more than equalled the population of the country villages taken as a whole. Religion, dislike of the sometimes rather arbitrary methods by which the Stuarts ruled, these were the burden of the speeches of members of Parliament.

" Soon there will be no liberties left in England," cried Master Gidding, one of the members for Ellington. But the real grounds on which the townspeople of the richer sort hated the Stuarts were different, and would not sound so well as this put into speech. For had Master Gidding spoken what was really in his mind he must have said this: " Soon there will be no liberty left in England for the rich men to do as they wish regardless of the interests of others, and for town merchants to buy and sell as they will, careless what damage results from their trade to the country in general, nor will there be liberty for the rulers of each district to arrange local affairs to suit themselves."

So the farce went on. The Puritan party in Parliament, in order to bend the King to their will, refused to grant taxes. In consequence the Navy decayed, pirates began to haunt the Channel, and the traders of England set up a howl against the King for failing to protect trade. Then, when Charles I collected ship money, apparently a perfectly legal customary due, not in the strict sense of the word a tax at all, these same merchants protested again, though the fleet so prepared did clear the Channel of the pests that had battened on English shipping.

The climax came when the Long Parliament was called. The members for Ellington went to Westminster determined upon certain things. The Star Chamber, that controlled the merchant, prevented abuses in local government, punished severely libel and sedition, must go. So, too, must the King's power of raising money without Parliament, for by means of that power Charles could at need carry on the ordinary peace-time Government without reference to the Commons. The House of Commons should as far as possible seize the reins of power from the King, and then, as the towns held a majority in the Commons, the views and interests of the merchant class would prevail in the government of the country.

To a point the country members were in agreement. They too found the control of the Star Chamber irksome, and the King's experiments in

New against Old

reviving feudal dues when taxes were refused had not pleased them. The average country member, however, unless he came from the eastern counties where Puritanism was strong, wanted no more than this. When the Puritan members went further and attacked the Church of England and the King's control of the Militia the Royalist party was formed.

On the whole Charles I was conciliatory. He gave up what he believed to be his undoubted rights at the demand of the Commons, only when they tried to deprive him of his power to protect the country, and attempted to disestablish and persecute the Church of England did he take the step of opening his first campaign.

Ellington, like most of the other towns of England, supported Parliament in the Civil War that followed, at least the leading men and the merchants who ruled the town did so. The opinion of the unprivileged was not asked, they were simply pressed into service whether they would or no. But there is reason to suppose that they were none too enthusiastic in the cause.

At any rate the armies so composed, pressed townsmen led by godly but incompetent tailors and cloth-mercers and shipowners, proved quite unsuitable, and it was the genius of Cromwell and his professional army that won the war for Parliament.

The English Town

Whereupon there was trouble in the ranks of the victors. For the wealthy Presbyterian merchant had no sort of use for the Independents, a sect who believed in freedom of worship, *except for the Church of England and Catholics*—that is, perhaps, 70 per cent. of the population of England. The Presbyterian wanted to establish his own religion by force, and would tolerate nobody, not even other Puritans. Further, the Lord General Cromwell showed no signs of establishing a Republic of the Venetian pattern, the ideal of the English townsman. Thus, when the second Civil War broke out, we find the Presbyterian merchants of Ellington in alliance with their old enemies the Cavalier squires of the neighbourhood. But Cromwell and Fairfax were too much for them, and with the execution of the King the dominance of Oliver Cromwell was assured, though he did not, in name take over the rule of England for three years yet.

CHAPTER XIV
Growing-pains

ENGLAND was fortunate that it was Oliver Cromwell and not one of his colleagues who succeeded in making himself ruler of England. For Cromwell, though a second-rate and unoriginal statesman, was at least a great administrator, and could keep the peace between the warring sects who would otherwise have reduced England to anarchy. His home policy was but that of Charles I, strong central rule with a subordinate Parliament, differing only in the matter of religion; and Cromwell had not Charles's sensitive conscience, and was more powerful, thus finding possible acts of high-handedness that Charles neither would nor could have committed. His foreign policy was a copy of that of Elizabeth—religious and commercial war with Spain, a policy by this time seventy years out of date. The man would have been great as a subordinate, carrying out the plans of a more original mind. As it was, Professor Gardiner points out, he almost left England bankrupt.

The towns that had opposed the King found

that they had exchanged the devil for the deep sea, and the deep sea of Cromwell's needs threatened to drain away all their wealth. For Cromwell, like Henry V and Napoleon, discovered that one very simple way of side-tracking discontent at home is by foreign war, and, like the other people I have mentioned, he only discovered too late that that method is very expensive and uncertain.

The merchants of Ellington pulled long faces enough when they discovered what they had done in destroying the rule of the King. For the taxes that they must pay to Cromwell were far higher than Charles had ever demanded, and raised with no more consideration for legality. Nor did Cromwell's foreign policy help to fill the pockets of the men of Ellington to enable them to meet his demands. They had been all in favour of war with the Dutch, dangerous competitors on the sea, but Cromwell's first act was to put a stop to that war and attack Spain.

This was popular enough at first. Merchants and shipowners rubbed their hands as they thought of the untold wealth that was to be got from Spanish galleons on Drake and Hawkins' lines. But disillusionment was swift and terrible. The wicked Spaniards had worked out quite an efficient convoy system, and it took a whole fleet action now to capture a few treasure-ships. When the expenses of the war had been paid there was little left over to line the pockets of English townsmen.

Then as the Protectorate went on the burden of taxation grew and grew. At first Cromwell had saved the pockets of those who might be expected to support him by the immoral expedient of confiscating and taxing his political opponents' property almost out of existence. But this could not go on for ever, and in the end Cromwell had to appoint major-generals to exact the taxes that he required. The opinion of the towns changed rapidly. There might be something to say for a king after all, and as soon as the dangerous Lord Protector was dead Ellington became suddenly and violently Royalist.

When Tumbledown Dick, the good-natured, easygoing Richard Cromwell, failed to hold his father's position, and General Monck proclaimed King Charles II, Ellington was relieved.

For the rule of Cromwell had not only touched the pockets of the wealthy, it had touched the lives of the poor even more harshly. The holidays and maypole dancing, Christmas feast, and Church Ales that had brought a little good cheer into the hard lives of the poorer classes had been sum-marily suppressed by the gloomy fanatics who ruled the land under the Lord Protector, and

M

although Cromwell himself probably disapproved
of a good many of the excesses of his followers he
was in no position to prevent them. The man who
had massacred his hundreds in Wexford for true
religion and virtue and killed his King for the same
cause could hardly intervene to save the maypole
and the poor man's plum porridge.

So the King enjoyed his own again, and Parliament met once more, after eleven years of weird
experiments in Parliament-making. But it was a
very different Parliament from the Long Parliament of Charles I. The country was sick of
Puritanism and all its works, there was real
enthusiasm for the new King among the common
people, who might have no say in elections, but
could make themselves objectionable if really
moved. Puritan candidates for Parliament found
it wiser to adopt Mr Punch's advice to those about
to marry,[1] and refrain from wooing the electors.
A Parliament met that was far more Royalist than
the King. Even Presbyterian Ellington found it
wiser to choose Royalist candidates suggested by
the Cavalier Earl of Ellington, and a good many of
the leading Presbyterians in the town suddenly
developed a liking for Church of England services.

In fact, but for the careless generosity of Charles,
there would have been a bitter persecution of

[1] "Don't!"

Puritans. As it was they were debarred from any influence in the town, for nobody might be a member of the corporation unless he would take the Sacrament according to the Church of England. The laxer Puritans of Ellington got over this by attending once or twice in the year, and getting a certificate from the clergyman of the parish stating that they had done so, and then going elsewhere or nowhere for the rest of the year, since their own services were declared illegal.

But the persecution was comparatively mild. Charles II had no love for religious, or any other tyranny. He was far more interested in promoting English sea-power and colonial development. It was during this reign that several Pennsylvanian families, who trace their origin to Ellington, migrated under the charter granted by King Charles II to William Penn.

The Church of England had been restored, but it had suffered, under Cromwell's rule, materially and spiritually. Such stained glass and other beauties as Edward VI had left to St Mary's Church were thoroughly destroyed by Cromwell's men, and its once beautiful interior now looked like a whitewashed barn. Spiritually, too, the decay had begun. There were great and good bishops and clergy in the Church, but the tone of the age was lax and materialistic, and the Church of

The English Town

England suffered accordingly in influence and moral fervour. The gospel of grab was now a strong competitor to the gospel of Christianity.

Material prosperity, however, was ebbing slowly and steadily away from such towns as Ellington. True, the successful Dutch wars of Charles II did something to stem the decay. But the vigorous colonial policy of the King rather hastened it, transferring the centre of English trade more and more to the West and Southern Atlantic ports. The burgesses of Ellington clamoured for war with France, partly on religious grounds, partly because war with France would benefit them far more than the peaceful colonization policy that Charles was pursuing. But that shrewd monarch had no intention of fighting France, for he had neither sufficient trained troops nor sufficient money for that game.

Then came the Plague. We call it the Plague of London, but there is no doubt that it did more harm outside the city in proportion to its violence. Certainly Ellington never recovered from its effects. The disease reduced the population of the town, and not for more than a century did it begin to increase again. The town was not dying, as some other old towns were, but it was stagnant. There was a steady industry, that of weaving. Shipbuilding and fishing still brought profit to the town, but the expanding trade of England was elsewhere.

Growing-pains

Opposition to the King began to raise its head again. This time, also, the grounds were ostensibly religious, but in reality there was a deep political motive behind the new party, who called themselves the Whigs. Easygoing though he was, it was found that King Charles II had no intention of being anybody's puppet. I know that he has been charged with being the puppet of Louis XIV of France, but many modern historians, with whose view I fully agree, consider that in that matter Louis, not Charles, was the dupe. However that may be, cunning politicians like Ashley Cooper, Earl of Shaftesbury, found that they could not govern the country in their own way using Charles as a figurehead.

Therefore they set up in opposition to the King, seeking to substitute for him a more pliable ruler who would allow a small group of nobles to rule England in his name. There was no intention of allowing democracy—that is, that everybody should share in the government. Parliament was to direct policy, but Parliament could be made a mere agency for carrying out the will of the ruling clique. The people of England, the unprivileged farm-labourers and town workmen, would have no share or say in the matter of choosing their rulers. But a small group of nobles alone could not hope for success. They therefore entered an alliance with the richer town merchants. Since the great nobles could, to some degree, control the country elections, and the town merchants to a much greater degree those in the towns, this alliance could rule England if only the power of the Crown could be reduced to a cypher.

So Ellington was enthusiastically Whig, at least that portion of Ellington that governed the town, reduced now to a very small group of rich men who had captured the organization of the decayed craft gilds, and filled their ranks with their own friends. For the gilds were no longer an active and living force in the town, only the name and outward form remained. Thus, the government of the town was in the hands of a few among its wealthier men, and the people of the town were helpless against them.

Fiery Protestantism, Parliamentary control of the Crown, and the substitution of the foolish, weak Duke of Monmouth, an illegitimate son of the King, for the strong James, Duke of York, the King's brother, as heir to the throne were the professed objects of this new party. Some were openly in favour of a republic.

So two new clubs came into existence in Ellington, a Green Ribbon Club of active Whigs, who drank the new-fangled coffee in a coffee-house set up by an enterprising citizen in Market Street, and discussed the prospects of their party, and a more select and secret body, the Calves' Head Club, of furious republicans, who solemnly ate a calf's head on the 29th of January in mockery of Charles I's murder, and talked a good deal of treason, such as would certainly have got them executed under the " mild and liberal-minded " Cromwell, but was wisely ignored by the " tyrannical " Government of Charles II.

What the common people of Ellington thought of this is not recorded. Many of them were Independents in religion or belonged to queer sects such as Fifth Monarchy men and Muggletonians, and were at intervals imprisoned for unlawful preaching, and let out again when the King was strong enough to defy the persecuting tendencies of his supporters. These were simple folk who believed the terrible tales of the town magnates, that the Papists were plotting to kill the King, make James King of England, and introduce the Inquisition into the country. So they would cry " No Pope " and " King Monmouth " with the rest. But there were many humble folk who went to church, prayed for the King, and would have been content with their lot but for the grasping domination of a clique of wealthy and unscrupulous men in the town. These regarded a strong king as their best protection in the battle of life, and were sincere, if powerless, supporters of the King. There were Tories, too,

The English Town

among the great men of the town, old-fashioned merchants who regarded with horror the hard business methods of the newer men, but they were in a minority, and destined to remain so for many years.

Then came the tales of Doctor Titus Oates, detailed accounts of a supposed Catholic plot to murder the King. How far the evil genius of Shaftesbury was behind this business it is hard to tell. Certainly the Whigs made the most of the story for their own purposes. In towns such as Ellington a perfect orgy of persecution began. Secret Catholics were dragged out and tried and hanged on stupidly false evidence. The town was in a panic. Men carried great wooden flails, " Protestant flails " to beat off the Catholic attack that was alleged to be coming. Terrible tales of the burnings in Mary's reign (there had been exactly two cases in Ellington) were revived with additions and extras. And the most degrading aspect of the whole affair is this, that half those who used the panic did not believe in it. Certainly Alderman Jenkins, an active Whig, must have suspected it, for this is how he writes:

> The horrid Popish plot is most opportune to our hand, for the King will scarce refuse the Exclusion Bill when all men believe the tales of Doctor Oates, whose credit, therefore, ought to be upheld by all supporters of liberty and the Protestant religion.

Growing-pains

Not the letter of an enthusiastic believer in Doctor Titus Oates, but Mr Alderman Jenkins is ready enough to use the scare for his own purposes. The King was too acute for the Whigs on this occasion. He would not proclaim his belief in the falseness of the whole affair and thus provoke the Protestant rebellion that the Whigs desired, but he waited quietly till the Whigs had made themselves unpopular, then he struck. Shaftesbury had to flee to Holland, and for a while Catholic and Protestant Dissenter alike were left in peace by the cynical King, who desired to persecute neither group as long as they on their side refrained from rebellion and tumult.

Then there descended on Ellington Mr Justice Jeffreys, a handsome, grim-faced man, to inquire into the terms by which the town held its charter. As might be expected, he found that in the course of centuries certain technical violations of the charter had taken place, and Ellington was compelled to accept another charter, securing a Tory mayor and corporation. For the moment the Whig plot was defeated, and Charles II ended his reign more powerful than his father had ever been, and popular, withal, for personal qualities.

If only James II had had his brother's political skill and tact the Whigs would probably have been defeated for ever. But he raised in an acute form the religious question, and that gave the Whigs their chance.

In Ellington the crisis took a sudden and acute form. For the last of the Stamner Earls of Ellington had died without heirs, and the title and property thus reverted to the Crown, since the old man had resolutely refused to will his property to the only relatives he had left, very distant cousins who had taken the Whig side in politics, and whom he therefore hated. James created a new earl, and gave him the property of the old earldom, which included a great deal of land around Ellington, and the new earl at once opened the old chapel of the castle and held service there according to the Catholic rite. There was a furious No Popery riot in the town, the chapel was burned by a raving mob, and a priest killed. Then in a rage James had the ringleaders of the riot, including John Bates, a leading shipbuilder of Ellington, arrested and hanged for riot.

Then came the abortive Monmouth rebellion, and finally the landing of the King's clever son-in-law, William of Orange, who had been plotting for years to seize the English throne. At last, sighed the Whigs, a king who will be ruled by *us* instead. They were mistaken, but after William's death they got what they wanted in George I. England had entered the period of the Whig Oligarchy.

CHAPTER XV
The Whig Oligarchy

THERE had been several motives affecting many people in the Revolution of 1688. The Tories, as a rule Royalists, had been frightened by James II's religious policy. It is almost certain that all James intended to do was to give those of his own religion a position of equality in England with others, the charges of intended persecution of all but Catholics are not supported by much real evidence. But genuine Church of England men were terrified of the very name of Rome, and accepted William of Orange as a lesser evil than the Pope. The great Whig nobles wanted a king whom they could govern.

As for the townsmen of Ellington their attitude is easy enough to discover. The Dissenters, and there were many of them, feared a Catholic king, even though he had proved more tolerant than a Protestant Parliament. The wealthy merchants were in alliance with the Whig nobles; they wanted England governed in their way and to their advantage, for even though the Star Chamber had been abolished, still the Stuarts would not give up their policy of refusing to consider class interests before those of the nation. As for the common people, " the mob " as the Whig called them when he was not touting for their support, they were not consulted. Not that this is surprising, for popular opinion is a vague and unsatisfactory guide to definite action, the people as a whole may have some clear idea as to what sort of thing they want, but, even to-day, practical details, the methods of securing these objects, are a matter for experts.

It is in national rather than local laws that the first results of Whig government make themselves apparent. A detailed and complicated system of protection is set on foot, but with little scientific basis behind it. Taxes on this and on that foreign commodity go on, but, unlike the modern believer in Protection, the Whig merchant class does not seem to have distinguished between what could be produced at home, and therefore, on Protectionist theories, ought to be taxed if imported, and what could not be produced at home and should therefore be imported freely. The Colonial policy of the Stuarts was allowed to lapse. For fifty years, the Navigation Acts, regulating trade with the Colonies, were not enforced, and such laws as the Statute of Apprentices and others designed for the protection of the poorer classes were simply allowed to die out.

The Whig Oligarchy

These proceedings added a new but not very creditable industry to those already established in Ellington. Since everything coming from abroad was heavily taxed it paid to smuggle, and smuggle the sea-faring folk of Ellington did. Nor was the offence regarded as serious by the non-smuggling population who bought the cheap goods offered by the smugglers. These, since the hand of the law was against them, the agents of the law very ready to shoot, and the punishments of a captured smuggler very severe (death if he had resisted the Preventative men, which smugglers did as a regular proceeding), became fierce and reckless fellows, defying not only the laws against smuggling, but all laws whatsoever. A quarter grew up down by the waterside of Ellington where a man could not safely walk after dusk, and even by day needed to pick his way with some care, especially if any chance action of his, some apparently innocent question, or a show of interest in what went on around him, should suggest to the inhabitants that he was a spy of the revenue authorities.

Altogether the town of Ellington by the days of William and Mary had changed very greatly from the thriving go-ahead city of the Middle Ages. The place seemed asleep. Weaving, manufacture of various articles for local consumption, and

189

fishing still flourished. The once great ship-building industry was dying, for Ellington was some way from the sea, and the new age demanded vessels of greater burden than could be launched into the river that flowed by the town, which was, in addition, silting up. A few fishing smacks and small coasters were still built in the yards by the river-bank, but many once prosperous ship-builders' wharves were now but tottering stages of rotting planks watching the river as an aged pensioner watches the life of his younger fellows pass by leaving him alone with his sad memories.

There were greater differences too between the homes and habits of the various classes in the town. Let us walk round it in imagination, and try and reconstruct Ellington as it was between the reigns of Queen Anne and George III.

The town, as has been explained, stood on a slight rise, and was dominated by a Norman castle set upon an artificial mound. The castle is still there, but the old grey stone with its aloof dignity is now marred by a huddle of dirty red-brick sheds clustered around its massive base. A utilitarian age has turned the fortress of the Malins and the Stamners into a town gaol. There is no Earl of Ellington now, the last died in exile with the King to whom he had clung through good report and ill, his last toast " To the squeezing of the Rotten

Orange!" So why not use their unwanted castle to house the unwanted prisoners of the town? There is little sentiment in this eighteenth century; hard heads, hard hearts, hard cash, these are the things on which Ellington and England in general pride themselves.

Below the castle is the Castle Square, where rank and fashion dwell. Neither are very exalted. Rank is represented by Sir Peter Casson, a worthy and wealthy shipowner, who has wisely retired from that business before it became a source of ruin rather than profit. After that a small cash transaction with an agent of Sir Robert Walpole has secured the knighthood that is the goal of the worthy man's ambitions. He is the Mayor of Ellington and recognized leader of local society.

Fashion is represented by his wife, his son, and his daughter. True, it is a little out of date, but roads were bad, and opportunities to go to London and see what is the latest mode few and far between. Lady Casson wears a stiff, much flounced silken robe, builds her hair into a much pomaded and insanitary bundle piled high over her head, and takes the air in a lumbering coach when not sitting reading, or pretending to read, the modish novels of Mr Richardson or Mr Fielding, or doing intricate and useless needlework. Her conversation consists largely of such expressions as " Oh, Lah!"

and " Oh, Lud! " (" Oh, Lord," would be deemed vulgar and common), and fifth-hand titbits of Court gossip. She is, as necessity demands, a virtuous Whig, and drinks to his Majesty and confusion to the Pretender. Her daughter is a prettier copy of herself, with even higher-piled hair and more elaborate flounces. She, however, apes the latest Court fashions, and is consequently always rather blue about the lips, and inclined to what she calls " the vapours " and to faint on very small occasion, which is not surprising to one who knows how tightly her waist is pinched.

Mr Horace Casson is a languid young gentleman, who in secret uses various preparations to retain the creamy complexion of his face, and clothes his slim body (he, like his sister, wears stays) in the most vivid-hued coats and knee-breeches. He wears a much-powdered wig and a small-sword, drinks a bottle of port wine a day (Sir Peter is old-fashioned and sticks to claret—three bottles), and contrives to do nothing at all. One day he will be member of Parliament for the free and ancient borough of Ellington. Meanwhile life is good enough.

One more house and we can leave the Castle Square and seek elsewhere in the town. This is the house of Colonel Rathbone, a quiet, flat-fronted house of old red brick. The rooms are furnished with the solid, sturdy furniture of a past day, the garden wild and careless, a contrast, and a deliberate contrast, to the formal Dutch garden of Sir Peter Casson. It would be best not to talk about Dutch gardens, or Dutch anything else to the Colonel, who potters about in his gaily broidered shirt-sleeves, for he has learned his language in the army of King Charles II, at Tangier, and any such tactless references will certainly provoke a spate of oaths.

But if you are not an obvious Whig the Colonel will receive you courteously, and invite you to drink with him. He will take you into his solid, oak-furnished study, and bring forth with reverent care a bottle of sound old wine. He will look cautiously at you, and if he decides that you are the right sort of man a bad landscape or portrait on the wall will be turned round, to disclose another picture, the melancholy, dreamy face of King James III of England, living now in exile at Rome. The Colonel raises his glass toward the portrait, passes it across a bowl of water, and murmurs as he drinks it, " The King." Then perhaps he will walk a little way on your road with you, bowing with old-fashioned grace to his friends. For everything about the Colonel is old-fashioned, including his large periwig. But let him meet Sir Peter or Mr Horace, and his lip curls, his hand

N

touches the hilt of his sword, and he stalks past them as if they did not exist. He made a good end, brave old Colonel Rathbone, riding north on a rumour that King James had landed in Scotland, though ordered by his physician to keep his bed. What matter that the rumour was false? He died in the service of the king to whom he had sworn allegiance as much as if he had fallen upon the battlefield.

Come a little lower down the hill, along Staple Street. This is a narrow, quiet road, with substantial houses on both sides of it. We will turn in at the house of Lawyer Tillet. Here in a front room sits the lawyer, surrounded by musty parchments, a little dry man, whose large head is covered by a little, dry-looking wig, very different from the flowing, exuberant wig that crowns the beauty of Mr Horace Casson.

Everything here is solid and sound. The furniture is worn but good, old-fashioned it is true, but not with deliberate purpose as in Colonel Rathbone's house. Good, solid chairs around a good, solid table, plenty of good but simple food and moderation of good wine—that is the lawyer's way of living. He is a prodigious snuff-taker, and among his cronies sometimes smokes a long churchwarden pipe. With these friends of his, Doctor Dawson and Mr Keech the bookseller, he

A CHOP-HOUSE IN THE EIGHTEENTH CENTURY

Dr Johnson, seated on the right, helps us to appreciate the table manners of the period.

From a satirical engraving by H. Bunbury.   194

sits each day in the coffee-house down the street, talking over the news of the day. Three of the solid, honest backbone of the Whig party these, to whom the British Constitution as established by the Act of Settlement is perfection itself, the Government of Robert Walpole and his successors all that could be desired, and Whig principles, liberty in Church and State (except, of course, for Papists, Tories, Jacobites, and such cattle), the best political creed ever invented. They are far more lovable men these than Sir Peter and his circle; they are honest, if a little dull, and do not pretend to be other than they are, hard-headed men of business, very well satisfied with their lives.

If you wish to find Mrs Tillet and Griselda, her daughter, you must make your way to the back of the house, through a great stone kitchen where, before an open fire, a joint roasts on the spit, and a red-faced cook busies herself with the preparation of dinner. Here you will find the still-room, and the two women at work over jars of preserves and pickles, or salting down a great ham. For Mrs Tillet is wont to say that she is no fine lady aping the doxies of the Court, but a good housewife, and will have her daughter brought up the same. Most of her clothes and her daughter's are home made, though Mr Tillet is generous, and now and then will buy them a costume from Hallet's, the modish shop in the High Street. Honest simplicity, care for the good things of this world, blindness to its evils, these are the main features of the lawyer's home.

Blind indeed these good people are. For we turn a corner out of this clean, homely street, very much the same then as it is to-day, and find ourselves back in the Middle Ages, only worse. Here is a foul, stinking court, a huddle of toppling buildings, with windows bricked up, till one shudders to think of the gloom of the rooms inside. There is a reason for that—windows are taxed. Here men, women, and children swarm in the filthy gutters, and the sanitary arrangements are those of the Middle Ages. There is no remedy, for the mayor is the owner of this slum, and since the Star Chamber has vanished there is no power in the land, short of an Act of Parliament, that can make him mend his ways, and as the Parliament is composed mainly of such men as Sir Peter, that is unlikely to be passed. These people are much worse off than their ancestors, for the open country is farther away from the centre of Ellington than then, and holidays, now that saints' days are disregarded, few and far between. Hours of work are long, wages low, and the Church, that might influence such men as Sir Peter, is fast asleep.

The Whig Oligarchy

If the pious builders of St Mary the Virgin's Church in Ellington could have risen from their tombs beneath its aisle and seen the state of their foundation they would have wept. Gone was the fine stained glass, gone the images of the saints. A number of high, square pews like horse-boxes surrounded a huge three-decker—a clerk's desk, a reading-desk, and a pulpit—shutting off any view of the beautiful east end of the old church. The walls are whitewashed, but the white is a courtesy adjective, it is slimy and grimy with neglect.

Here Parson Akers holds service on Sundays at eleven, or later if Sir Peter Casson should oversleep himself, for Parson Akers will not begin service without him. The congregation consists of a few of the gentry of Ellington who come as a fashionable exercise, and a cluster of servants and dependants who are sent.

" The lower classes *need* religion, y'know."

To these Parson Akers drones the service for morning prayer, and reads a sermon, if sober, which he sometimes is not. On such occasions the clerk announces that Parson Akers has the megrims, and the congregation disperses with a sigh of relief. Three times a year, as the law demands, a hurried Communion service is recited to the clerk and the mayor and corporation, who thus qualify to hold their offices, for the Test Act is still in force. Otherwise the church stands empty and silent.

Poor Parson Akers, drunken, disreputable, infidel priest of the Church, it is not altogether his fault, but the fault of his times. The keen, honest clergy of the Church of England are in the main Tories, suspected of being Jacobites. For them there are no parishes to be had, for most of the patronage is in the hands of rich Whig nobles or merchants, and they have no intention of allowing the Church to be used to upset their dominance in the State. So the stupid, dissolute younger son, who will recite a meaningless form of words once a week for an easy living, gets the parishes, except here and there in the country, where a Tory squire presents a living to some lean-jawed, fierce-eyed priest, who preaches on passive obedience and the wickedness of rebellion, and holds a solemn service of mourning for King Charles the Martyr on the 29th of January each year. Other parishes there are in charge of some learned and Whiggish divine, who, indeed, does his best, but fears enthusiasm or keenness, the hall-mark of the Jacobite on one side or the ranter on the other.

However, a whirlwind sweeps through Ellington during this period, a tall man with a strong, kindly face who preaches in alleys and in the market-place " Repent ye, for the Kingdom of Heaven is at hand." John Wesley comes to Ellington, bringing religion into dark, neglected corners, convicting men of sin, urging them to decent living. He has the faults of the Puritan strain in his make-up, the narrowness, the hatred of harmless pleasure, but at least he is honest and loyal to his Master, and goes to seek the sheep that their paid shepherds have lost and do not even want to find.

Soon there are two centres of living religion in Ellington, the mean house in a mean street where Wesley's followers meet, and the plain little chapel, furnished by the bounty of Colonel Rathbone, where the few Roman Catholics of Ellington assemble.

Such is Ellington during the reign of the Whigs, and indeed for some time after. A sordid, dull age, stagnant and heavy-witted, after the stress and storm of the seventeenth century. Every man for himself and the devil take the hindmost is the creed of the average man—that is if he believes in the devil at all, and has not been reading the works of fashionable and rather naughty philosophers who disprove religion and virtue, and all the silly old superstitions of former ages.

That this was due to the system of government of which the next chapter has to tell cannot be doubted. In exchange for the tyranny of a king we now have the far worse tyranny of a small group, worse because very often the king's arbitrary acts were meant for the good of the country as a whole, while it is very rare that a body of men can be induced to forget their own interests and consider those of other people.

CHAPTER XVI
Local Government

ONE can imagine the life of Georgian Ellington: the brocaded gentlemen and silken ladies walking mincingly along the rough pavements of Castle Square ; the long solemn dinners where port and sherry flowed like water, the occasional duels between two young bucks over a lady's favours, the gang of elegant young roughs who, in imitation of the Mohawks and other rowdy London youths, upset watchmen in drunken frolic.

One can imagine the solemn tradesmen attending the drunken ministrations of Parson Akers or his like, or going solemnly each Sunday to hear a service at some dissenting chapel of one of the older sects. One can imagine them piling money on money, well content with a Government that did not interfere with them save in case of flagrant fraud, when punishment was swift and severe.

At the other end of the scale, one can imagine the huddle of porters, sedan-chair bearers, honest workmen, dishonest rascals, who swarmed and bred in the poorer quarters of the town. For them the Government was a harsh, fierce enemy, and well they knew what they had to fear.

A cart comes down the street from the town gaol, containing three trembling wretches and the Reverend Mr Akers, praying with unctuous vigour. A cheering, jeering mob watches the procession. Here are two wretched fellows who, driven mad by hunger, have broken into a food shop, and a highway robber who has more murders to his account than he can remember. God help them, for the penalty is the same, hungry thief and murderous outlaw, both must be choked slowly to death by an unskilful hangman. The only difference between their fates is that while the friends of the two poor thieves may have their bodies to bury, the highway robber must hang in chains.

Or, on another day, a woman stands, half-stripped, chained to a tall post while the same savage hangman lashes her bleeding flesh. She has been caught in some offence that to-day would be met by a fine or at the most a week in gaol.

A savage age, in some ways more savage than the Middle Ages, for property is its god, and offences against property are punished with a heartless severity that the tyrannical monarchs of the Middle Ages would not have countenanced.

One can imagine all these things, one can sit in the coffee-house of Ellington, listening to the talk

A CONDEMNED CRIMINAL ON HIS WAY TO THE GALLOWS

Showing the unseemly scenes of popular interest and excitement that accompanied executions.

From an engraving by Hogarth.

A Georgian Town Scene from Hogarth

Local Government

of the easygoing men who gather there to read the *Advertiser* or the *Intelligencer*, badly printed, often scurrilous rags of newspapers. One can imagine the eager panic with which those papers were scanned when Charles Edward marched to Derby, with what cruel relish when his followers were butchered upon Culloden Moor or executed upon Tower Hill or at Tyburn.

What is difficult for us in these days, when many hold that Government has gone to the limit or beyond it in fussy regulation of other folks' lives, is to imagine how these things were allowed to go on without effective protest. There seems to our minds to be no authority able and willing to right anything that might be wrong with the state of England.

In truth, when the country got rid of the Stuarts they got rid of the monarchy as the governing force of the country. But they failed to transfer the effective force of government to Parliament; indeed, many acute thinkers are now beginning to doubt if this can ever be done. Parliament can criticize, and it can reject the schemes of the Government, it can control the Government by refusing supplies, but it cannot originate policies, and we are still seeking an impartial and efficient authority to do so. What actually happened in the Revolution of 1688 was that the power of the

Crown was transferred to a group of ministers acting in name under the control of Parliament. How far that control was real we shall see in a moment.

In local affairs the same thing happened. In the country local government was in the hands of the Justices of the Peace, and they were chosen in name by the King, in fact by the leader of the political group that controlled the Crown, in this case the Whig families, and of course were mainly of the same political faction.

In the towns the mayor and corporation did what the Justices did in the country. Now the mayor and corporation were elected by the freemen of the towns, and should, therefore, in theory have been more independent of the Government. In fact they were even worse than the Justices of the Peace. For it must be remembered that trade and commerce had moved, but the chartered boroughs who returned members to Parliament and elected their own mayor and corporation were still the same as in the Middle Ages.

In some cases—for instance, Dunwich—this led to the return of members of Parliament for towns that no longer existed. The owner of the land where they had once stood—in the case of Dunwich, a desolate strip of coast, for the town was under the sea—returned himself or anybody he chose as a member of Parliament. That was known as a 'rotten borough.'

But Ellington was more typical of what had happened to the old towns of England. Trade and population had been stagnant for a century, and the gilds had all but vanished. In name, however, they still existed, but their membership was confined to a few wealthy men who could pay high fees for their election, and these, and these only, had any say in the choice of the mayor and corporation and the two members that Ellington returned to the House of Commons.

Nor were the freemen of the town themselves free to choose as they would in this matter. For they were most of them tradesmen, not manufacturers, dependent on Lord Astwood, who had bought up most of the land round Ellington, and on his friends for the main part of their profits of trade. Therefore they could not refuse his requests, and the members for Ellington really represented Lord Astwood.

Nor was this the worst feature of the business from the town's point of view. This little clique was not only out of touch with the interests of the poorer classes, but there was a direct conflict of interest, far greater than between the landowner and the farm-labourer in the country.

What the mayor and corporation needed most

was cheap labour and high profits, while the others wanted, of course, cheap food and high wages, and there was no impartial authority to see fair play between the two parties, forcing each to subordinate their selfish demands to the common good. The power of the Crown, backed by the Star Chamber, had been such an authority. Now that was gone, and where were the losers in the conflict of interests to look for justice? Certainly not to Parliament, which was composed in the main of the very class that was oppressing them. True, the Tory party was prepared to do something for the town labourer, especially for the terribly oppressed factory labourer, mainly because the Tories disliked and wanted to annoy the Whig traders and manufacturers. But they were weak and powerless, and when they gained power the French Revolution threw all schemes of social reform (and Pitt certainly *had* such schemes) into the political dustbin, the more as the merchant, frightened lest revolution should spread to England, turned Tory for the nonce, and his influence swamped the party.

Now the town Government had in their hands certain powers that could be used to their own profit, and to the great loss of other classes. Chief of these was the Poor Law system. By that the relief of the poor and the punishment of the

Local Government

vagrant were left in the hands of the Justices of the Peace, that is, in Ellington, in the hands of Sir Peter Casson, Parson Akers, and such men as these. They frankly used those powers to their own advantage, and nobody could prevent them doing so.

This they could do in several ways. Chief among them was the scheme of employing paupers at a low wage, and paying the rest of their wages out of the rates.

Another example of this sort of swindle is as follows: a certain John Deering of Ellington was the owner of a small cottage for which no one would pay any rent, so vile and ruinous was it. But John Deering was also one of the overseers of the poor and a Justice of the Peace, and it was his duty to administer relief to paupers. So this thrifty man established a family of paupers in his tumbledown hovel, charged them ten shillings a week in rent, a shocking price even had the cottage been in good repair, and, since the paupers could not of course pay, took the money out of the poor rate that he, as overseer, collected.

Pauper children, too, were abominably misused. The wretched infants were apprenticed to tradesmen of the town, who were allowed to ignore entirely the clause in the indenture that bound them to teach their apprentices their trade. The pauper apprentice was simply an unpaid, half-starved drudge. Sometimes there was a scandal that moved even the harsh mayor and corporation to action, as when a certain William Wright, a bonnet-maker and draper of Ellington, whipped a clumsy pauper-girl apprentice till she fainted, and then threw her, without her clothes, into a dark cellar, where the miserable child hanged herself in terror and madness with a piece of rope that she found upon the floor of her prison. Wright was sent to gaol for a year, but the scandal still went on. Again the fault was lack of any central authority strong enough to control the local despots and make them realize their responsibilities.

Bribery and corruption too were rampant in the town, though here the townsfolk were but following the lead of their betters. " Every man has his price," said the cynical Sir Robert Walpole, and on that principle he conducted the government of the country. " This country cannot be governed except by corruption " was the opinion of another eighteenth-century statesman, and even the honest William Pitt, Earl of Chatham, had to employ the Duke of Newcastle to manage the corruption of the electorate for him.

In the matter of electing members to Parliament the corrupting of the freemen of Ellington was carried out on approved lines. Threats and cash down were both used. In the first place, a freeman who voted against the nominee of Lord Astwood would, as has already been explained, lose the custom of the lord and his friends, which meant ruin. There were perhaps half a dozen freemen, small manufacturers whose trade was not purely local, whom such threats did not affect, but they, even if they did oppose the lord's nominee, were powerless. Then there was free beer at election time for all voters who did as they were told, free meals at the candidate's expense, and a five-pound note to those who behaved themselves. Voting was open, so that it was perfectly easy to tell who had voted as expected, and who had not.

Municipal elections were managed in exactly the same way. Only the little knot of freemen had any say in the election of the mayor and corporation of Ellington, and they were easily managed. True, one impudent fellow, a small manufacturer of woollen goods, had the audacity one year to propose the election to the corporation of two independent freemen, men who, in disgust at the way things were run, had always refused to record a vote at all. That matter was simply dealt with. John Higgins, the man in question, was a hard though just employer; there would be no free beer for his supporters, so that the mob could easily be

o

turned against him. It must be realized that, though the common people had no vote, it was always worth a candidate's while to make them drunk and merry at his expense. Then they would cheer him and applaud his futile speeches, but if not they would more than probably break up his meetings and generally make themselves disagreeable.

So a little money transaction with one Jasper Kew, a smuggling rascal with a persuasive tongue, put Mr Higgins out of action. He would supply no free beer for the people of Ellington; indeed, he was no believer in beer at all, it interfered with his one idol, hard work. It was, therefore, no difficult task for Jasper Kew to lead on a howling, half-tipsy mob to set fire to Higgins' factory, a wooden shed in a patch of waste land just outside the town. Mr Mayor sympathized greatly with Mr Higgins, and would surely punish the scoundrels who had done this thing if they could be found, but, strange to say, all the efforts of the town authorities could not trace the criminals.

What the rulers of the town did, of course, every petty Jack-in-office imitated. The town council too were of a thrifty turn of mind, and one cannot altogether blame an underpaid beadle or constable if he took what he could get from his office. Even the executioner expected a tip from his victims,

and woe betide the wretch sentenced to be hanged
or whipped who failed to pay. The executioner
would bungle his work, or lay on the lash with
extra vigour, and the man or woman would have
ample cause to regret their meanness or poverty.

Naturally, such a corporation was unlikely to
interfere with bad landlords, harsh employers of
labour, and others who did damage to the town's
interests to fill their pockets, for it depended
largely on such men for its existence. And upon
its own dunghill the corporation was the only
rooster, the discontented could get up petitions
to Parliament or even to the Privy Council if it
amused them to do so. One would not and the
other could not interfere. Life was very hard
indeed in the towns of England for all but the
well off, harder probably than in the country, for
though agricultural wages were very, very low
there were usually some extras, a vegetable garden,
a few pickings from the employer's farm, perhaps
cheap milk to ease the poor man's burden. Also,
on the whole the old-fashioned country squire was
a better employer than the town manufacturer or
shopkeeper. He might be a drunken, swearing,
boot-throwing, horse-whipping rascal, but the
country squire had not yet lost the older tradition
that he was in some degree responsible for his men,
as the town employer had, and if the country

labourer lived in a ghastly hovel, at least he worked and his children played in the fresh air, not in the stale and stinking atmosphere of an Ellington court or close.

Perhaps in the matter of amusement the town labourer suffered most as compared with the countryman. For the wealthy there were routs, balls, parties, and sometimes a company of strolling players in the town. For the poor there was the gin-shop, where, as one or two advertised, " A man might be drunk for a penny and dead drunk for twopence." One even added the allurement, " Clean straw provided." The old happy festivals that all classes had shared, the dancing around the maypole, the Church Ales, the saint's day festivals, all had vanished in the towns, though in the country there were still some remnants, May Day and Harvest Home, to cheer the hearts of the poorer folk.

The eighteenth century was, indeed, no time for a poor man to be born and die, and the Industrial Revolution, with which we are now to deal, at first seemed to make matters worse.

CHAPTER XVII

The Industrial Revolution and Reform

WHAT we know as the Industrial Revolution was a long, slow process, beginning at some period about 1700 and continuing until the middle of the nineteenth century. It marks the change from the older England, a country mainly agricultural, whose chief exports were raw materials, wool, and hides, to a country mainly urban, whose people live largely on the making up of raw material into goods salable not only at home but abroad. We can see the change that has taken place if we consider that England was in the Middle Ages a wheat-exporting country, whereas after the Industrial Revolution we imported most of the wheat required to feed our growing population. Before the Industrial Revolution the population of England did not much exceed ten millions, about the greatest number that can be fed successfully on home produce alone. Now it exceeds forty millions.

To Ellington the Industrial Revolution brought many changes. First came the finding of a seam of coal under Squire Worral's land just outside the boundaries of the town. At once every ambitious man in Ellington was on the Squire's doorstep with offers of untold wealth, for now coal was money. Men had discovered how iron might be worked by means of coal, and the whole face of the middle of England was scarred and marred by coal-pits and iron-works. But iron was common enough in the country round Ellington, and had, in fact, been worked in a desultory fashion for centuries. With this new discovery the languishing trade of the town might be revived. Squire Worral's reply to overtures was coarse and to the point.

He would see the rich men of Ellington, and their mothers and grandmothers, and their children to the remotest generations fried for ever in the lowest regions of hell before he would sell them an acre of his land, or the right to burrow under it. Wasn't the clean sky good enough for them that they must dirty it with their smoke; weren't the forests that God had planted good enough that they must go digging under the earth for things to burn? And anyhow he was going to have no dirty coal-digging, no smoky iron-works within his borders, and much more of the same sort.

The Squire meant well. He loved his land and those who lived on it, and had the name of a kindly, easy master, but he loved also the ruby glow of wine, the green allure of the card-table, and he would spend his last penny and over on either. Thus it happened that when the old Squire died the land must be sold to pay his debts, and the sinking of the coal-mine was begun.

It brought new life to the trade of Ellington, and much wealth to the enterprising men who provided the capital. It also reduced the burden of unemployment, and thus the poor rate entailed by the host of unemployed. But conditions of labour in the mines were worse than in the factories that now began to spring up when cheap coal was available. For that the employers were not altogether to blame, engineering science had not yet discovered how to avoid the dangers of badly ventilated pits and the deadly coal damp.

But the terrible hours of work, the use of tiny children as pit-carriers, and the cheap and nasty material that was used in constructing props, cages and other appliances on which the safety of the workers depended was due to nothing but the petty greed of dull, uneducated men whose sole capacity was that of getting money more quickly than their fellows, or to something worse. For when a horrible disaster due to the breaking of a cage rope led to certain investigations, it was found that a respected citizen, Walter Noyer, a marine-store dealer of Ellington, had supplied the cheapest and worst quality of rope while taking money for a better quality, with the connivance of a manager employed by the Ellington coal-mines.

The finding of coal brought, as I have said, changes to the manufacturing life of Ellington. That same John Higgins, who had protested so vigorously against the corruption of the clique that governed Ellington, took advantage of the cheap supply of coal now available to install steam in his cloth factories.

For during the period that has been described certain inventions had been made that enabled machinery to do what had before needed the skilled hands of practised workers. 'Spinning Jenny' had strangled the cottage industries, and her numerous children were slowly completing the process. England was becoming a land of crowded towns and factories. It seemed too at first that these new inventions would result in a diminution of the population, for one machine could do the work of ten men. So thought the workers of Ellington town; and there was rioting and attempted destruction of John Higgins' machinery. Eventually soldiers had to be called out to suppress the trouble.

However, the factory was started, and no sooner was it in working order than certain facts came to light. Hours of work were fourteen or more in the day, wages but a few shillings a week. Children of five or six years old were employed for twelve hours a day in the weaving-rooms, and beaten into activity with a leather thong. The curious thing is that withal Higgins was an honest man, humane, in his own way, and even benevolent. There was no keener member in all Ellington of the newly formed association for the Abolition of Slavery, no preacher in the chapel he attended who could speak with more soul-stirring fervour of the woes of the ' Black Brother.' The man simply did not see that there was anything inconsistent in his slave-driving at home and slave-freeing abroad.

Not that the horrors of this factory were all new, or all due to Higgins himself. But the herding together of the victims in a factory brought the facts out into the open. The children who toiled and wept in the factory had worked as hard in their own homes, and, vilely insanitary as the factory was, it was no worse than those homes. Nor were the hours longer in the factory than in the older domestic industry of the late seventeenth and early eighteenth centuries, but they were far longer than would have been tolerated by the medieval gild, or the ' tyrannical ' Stuart regulations, and, taking into account the increased cost of living, the wages were not up to the standard of an earlier day. The simple truth was that lack of central control had resulted in a sort of industrial feudalism, quite as oppressive as the unrestrained feudalism of France under the weak rulers of the Middle Ages, when every baron oppressed his serfs at will.

Yet, like other seeming tragedies, the Industrial Revolution led to certain good effects. Just as the South Sea Bubble a generation earlier had brought to light the danger of the joint-stock company, and forced the Government to step in against their own professed principles of leaving the money-getter to acquire his wealth how he would, and regulate this form of commerce, so the Industrial Revolution brought certain evils into the open. Men could ignore, either through wilful blindness or real lack of knowledge, overwork, child-slavery, starvation wages, brutality to apprentices, and so forth, as long as these things were done in isolated cottages, and as long as news travelled slowly over muddy, rutted roads. But when these things were done openly in factory and coal-mine, and when the new, swift stage-coaches enabled men to travel up and down England, concealment was no longer possible.

The result is a very curious political alliance on one point and one point only. There were two groups of men who denounced these things,

Industrial Revolution and Reform

though the remedies they suggested were by no means the same. There was the new party, the Radicals, who argued that the " Cure for democracy is more democracy "—in other words, that since the deposition of strong central authority and the substitution of a Parliament based on a limited vote had led to these horrors, a Parliament, in the election of which everybody had a voice, would cure them. The other party who denounced this state of affairs were the High Tories, the old landed gentry and the older nobles, who, now that Bonnie Prince Charlie was dead, were willing to accept the rule of George III. Of course they regarded the Radical remedy as mere quackery. Their idea was a strong Tory Government that would tell the moneyed men of the towns to mend their ways with some speed or suffer the consequences.

It is a thousand pities that the High Tory remedy was never tried, for it might have succeeded. It is true that under a Parliament elected as the Radicals suggested these horrors have been all but abolished, but by a slow and clumsy process that has apparently made the struggle between Capital and Labour a permanent and very disquieting feature of our political life, and has, for reasons to be explained later, done a great deal of damage to English industries. A powerful reforming Government that was sure enough of its position and sufficiently independent of popular prejudices to do unpopular things, if need be, might have made a better hand of the business.

But it was not to be. The Napoleonic Wars broke out, and the High Tory enthusiast for better things had for a time to hide his head. The very suggestion of change was regarded as dangerous when what had begun as a real attempt at reform, supported by the King of France himself, had ended in bloody revolution that threatened to spread all over Europe. The necessity of repressing dangerous demonstrations formed and fixed the character of the Tory Party for a generation, and after the war their attempts at reforming industrial conditions were timid and feeble.

Such was the state of affairs in the nation during the trying years between 1789 and 1832. For Ellington the years were tumultuous and terrible. Riot and scare were their keynotes. First, as has been told above, came the riots against machinery. These died down when the chaos of Europe made England the trade centre of the world, and even on the low wages of the time a man could earn enough to exist, and when the flow of orders gave work to such an extent that the machines were employing as many as the older hand methods had employed. Only those on the outskirts of the

Industrial Revolution and Reform

town who had managed small farms and made up their living by hand-weaving were utterly ruined, for they neither could nor would take to machinery, and the little farming they did would not support them, especially now that new discoveries in agriculture had made capital and scientific management as necessary in that calling as in industry.

But the respite was very short. Europe fell under Napoleon's sway, the market for English manufactures contracted, the price of food soared and soared. Soon there were mobs in Ellington streets threatening the bakers' and butchers' shops, shrieking for food, and among them crept sly and persuasive agitators, egging them on to violence.

That was when Johnson the wheelwright became a power in the town. He chalked the tricolour over his door and under it the inscription, "Liberty, Equality, and Fraternity," the war-cry of red revolution. He preached to the starving, discontented mobs of the town.

"Get votes," he would shrill in his high, reedy voice. "Votes is power. Get the government of this town and of this country into your own hands, then bread will be at a penny a loaf and no man need starve, for there will be work for all!"

Like most of his kind, Johnson was conveniently vague as to the exact method by which this miracle was to be worked, but hungry men do not look very deeply into promises that their stomachs shall be filled. In truth, Johnson had visions of himself as Mayor of Ellington, Member of Parliament, even, perhaps, Prime Minister, or President of England. The man was eaten up with vanity. Yet he was no humbug. He did sincerely pity the wretchedness of his fellows, and felt, rightly, that the Government of England and of the town would do nothing. Neither threats nor prison had the least effect.

There were Johnsons in every town of England, and by the time that peace came, bringing yet worse misery, for the markets of Europe were disorganized, those of America as yet undeveloped, and the temporary employment provided by the needs of Wellington's army at an end, these men had convinced the discontented that in Parliamentary and Municipal reform lay their one hope of redress.

So began a new period of riots. Crowds clamoured in the streets again, but this time not against machinery or for bread, but for votes. The mayor and corporation of Ellington looked at one another. What were they to do? To give way meant their own ruin, to resist, riot. The same feeling pervaded the House of Commons. They too would do nothing but sit stubbornly on their rights and cry, " No change."

TROOPS FIRING UPON THE MOB DURING THE GORDON RIOTS

From a drawing by F. Wheatley.

222

THE CHAMPIONS OF REFORM ENTERING THE HOUSE AFTER THE
PASSAGE OF THE REFORM BILL OF 1832

The Duke of Wellington and other Tories are watching the arrival of William
Cobbett and Francis Place.

From a cartoon by J. Doyle.

223

Industrial Revolution and Reform

Now was the chance for some great spirit in town or country to take the lead, to say to the discontented, " No need to clamour for votes, we know what ills you suffer from and will take steps to right them."

But no voice came. On one side were the Tory politicians, demoralized by a long spell of power and by the fact that the revolutionary scare had attracted to their ranks all the commercial selfishness of eighteenth-century England, still a living force in the nineteenth century, refusing all compromise; on the other side the Whigs, hungry for office, seeking to make capital out of the country's discontent.

Here was their chance. Not only the working men of England were dissatisfied. There were thousands of well-off men in the Midlands and North, manufacturers thrown into wealth and power by the swift industrial development of those regions, who had little or no voice in Parliament because the towns where they dwelt were new-born affairs, without charters, returning no members to Parliament. There were men of some importance and position in chartered towns who could not secure the freedom of their towns and thus the right to vote. Here was the Whig chance to attract to their side once more the commercial men of England by producing a Reform

Bill, that, while falling far short of the expectations of the Radical party, would satisfy the demands of more moderate men. That they would have the population in general on their side was certain, for the belief that an extension of the franchise would lead inevitably to social reform was deep-rooted, and men who often could neither read nor write would hardly be able to fathom the real nature of the reform offered by the leader of the Whig party, Lord John Russell.

There was much agitation on both sides. The Whigs accused the Tories, with some truth, of being mere stick-in-the-mud fellows who would neither do anything themselves nor allow anyone else to do anything. The Tories retorted, also with some truth, that the Whigs were mere scheming politicians, whose sole object in urging reform was to transfer the power of electing Parliament to that class which might be trusted to vote Whig, and thus once again establish themselves in permanent power, as they had done in the days of Walpole.

Of course the truth was that all sorts of men co-operated both in advocating and opposing reform. There were among the Tories mere reactionaries who hated change, there were selfish men who feared that their own interests would suffer, and there were honest men who believed, and their belief is by no means ridiculous, that to make Parliament more dependent on popular opinion would be to make strong and efficient government impossible.

On the other side were selfish politicians who hoped that in gratitude for reform the new voters would make the Whig party the permanent Government of England. There were selfish men who hoped to secure their own interests through a Parliament that they would be able to control, and there were honest enthusiasts, like Lord Macaulay, the historian, who wanted reform for its own sake, because they believed that it would be for the good of the country.

The repressive measures of the Tory Governments since the Napoleonic Wars had frightened their merchant-class supporters. These were especially bitter against the system of protection of English corn supplies that the Tories had introduced for the benefit of English agriculture, for the townsman wanted cheap food, and cared little whether the country squire suffered in consequence. So in the House of Commons of 1832 the Whigs obtained a majority, though not a large one, and passed through the House a bill that gave the right to vote to substantial householders in the towns, and in the country to substantial landholders although they might not be freeholders. Besides

P

this, rotten boroughs and tiny, decayed towns that had returned members to Parliament ceased to do so, and in their place big and important towns, hitherto unrepresented, now sent one or more members to Parliament.

This was followed by a Municipal Reform Bill that established one general system of choosing the mayor and corporation of corporate towns instead of the hundreds of local customs hitherto in vogue. This was that every householder should have a vote in the choice of a corporation, which should then choose one of its members to act as mayor.

Ellington thus lost one of its members of Parliament, and the few families who had governed the town as their private preserve were compelled to admit others to a share in the work. This was certainly a little better than the old corrupt system, but to everybody's surprise the condition of the poor remained exactly as it had been before. The new Government in country and town proved no more accommodating in that matter than the old.

CHAPTER XVIII
Yesterday

WE have come to the nineteenth century, perhaps the most amazing in English history, yet one that no history book can treat fully for its events have not yet worked themselves out. I can give a very good example of that. When the Reform Bill of 1832 was passed the Whigs said that it was the final act of reform, there would be no more extension of the vote. The Tories laughed, and quite truly prophesied that once started the franchise must be extended to every man in the country, and we know now that the Tories were right. What we do not know is this, were the Tories also right in arguing that the result of that extension would be to make Parliamentary government impossible? To that question no conclusive answer can come for many years yet, and any suggested answer must be a matter of political opinion, A's opinion being worth exactly as much or as little as B's.

That is just one example of the difficulty that confronts the student of our immediate past. There are others even more formidable. We are

227

now suffering or enjoying the consequences of many policies and events of the last century, and it is difficult, indeed, to judge the real value of those events, as difficult as it would be for a boy to write an essay on the value of fruit as a food while either gorging himself with it or suffering from stomach-ache as a result of too much indulgence. In the first case the essay would be idiotically prejudiced in favour of fruit, in the second idiotically prejudiced against it.

Still, from the mass of material certain unbiased facts can be extracted. We can see the gradual changes that take place in English town life during the long era of Queen Victoria, though we cannot yet estimate their eventual consequences to our own lives.

Look once more at Ellington in the middle of the nineteenth century. The town is very little changed in outward show. The castle stands, desolate and deserted now, for no longer does Ellington possess a town gaol and around it the smug Georgian respectability of Castle Square. Lower down in the town we shall find some ancient Elizabethan houses, carefully plastered and whitewashed to make them tone in with the drab respectability of the rest of the town. The slums are there too, tottering and stinking as before, and still it is nobody's business to deal with them.

Yesterday

Charitable men and women do their best, but the local Government will not offend its most influential supporters by putting into force Acts of Parliament that have been passed with the idea of remedying the slum problem. The central Government will not enforce their own laws, for any interference by the Queen's Government with the rights and duties of locally elected aldermen and councillors is at once denounced as " Star Chamber tyranny." The belief that an elected body can do no wrong, and that the greater the number of electors the greater the infallibility of the elected is the beginning and the end of English Liberal belief. Even cynical, clever men like the brilliant Jew, Benjamin Disraeli, who is slowly becoming a leading force in the Tory party, though they have no belief in the system, have to make what use of it they can.

There is, however, a new building at the edge of the town, a railway-station, where slow and clumsy trains come snorting to the platform from distant London, doing the journey in no more than five hours. The old coaches took a full long day about it. Ellington is far less local and provincial than it was. The railway-train, though still distrusted by old-fashioned folk, will bring the London daily papers to Ellington by midday, and a manufacturer might have an office in

The English Town

Ellington and another in London, and travel to and fro once a week if he needed to do so.

That has led, of course, to an expansion of trade. First canals and then railways have enabled Ellington to send iron and woollen goods all over Europe, not, of course, on the scale of Birmingham or Bradford, but still, there is a thriving trade in such things. Thus new factories have been built on the outskirts of the town, and around them new slums of red brick back-to-back houses, run up by speculative and dishonest builders.

But the conscience of England was beginning to wake up. There were better types of capitalist here and there, men who considered the welfare, physical and moral, of their men, who had captured some of the spirit of older England, and treated their men well. There were others too, chief among them Lord Shaftesbury, who had worked and were working to better the condition of the labourer. Strange commentary on the hopes held out by the Whigs of a generation before. Shaftesbury and his followers were for the most part rigid High Tories! In truth the age-old tradition of the best type of English aristocrat was beginning to revive again after a century of gross materialism and selfishness. For Radicals like John Bright and Cobden were bitterly opposed even to such attempts at regulating conditions

AN EARLY NINETEENTH-CENTURY STREET FAIR

In this drawing Rowlandson commemorates the famous Rag Fair near Whitechapel, London, where old and worn clothing was vended to the inhabitants of that squalid district.

and hours of labour in factories and workshops as were made, chiefly by the more enlightened type of Tory. They stuck rigidly to the old Whig policy of allowing employer and employed to fight out their battles as best they might.

Such was the town of Ellington nearly a hundred years ago. Gone were the gay Georgian bucks. In their place solemn, bewhiskered men in top-hats and black coats hurried through the streets. Rank and fashion had migrated to London. A few great men lived in country seats outside the town when not abroad or in London, but the town itself was given up to those who had business therein. Down in the poor quarters drabness became squalor. Clothes were dirty without being picturesque; the cast-off frock-coat of the Victorian gentleman covering the ragged back of a casual labourer had by no means the raffish gaiety of the cast-off red and purple coat of a Georgian man about town. Smoke was king, dulling every hue down to its own drab solemnity, and drab solemnity was the keynote of the town's life.

In outward show St Mary's Church is as it was in good King George's day—whitewash, three-decker, parish clerk, all are there. But the Reverend Mr Akers and all his kind are vanished. The Reverend Silas Connington is Vicar of Ellington now, a lean, solemn-faced man of middle age, terrible in his wrath, whose sermons on sin and hell fire are positively frightening. No relaxation will he allow to sinful humanity. A pack of cards is the devil's prayer-book, a theatre the ante-chamber of hell, a novel the tempter's own favourite snare, and dancing the very worst of Satan's devices for ruining humanity. Sunday is a day of humiliation and gloom. Those who follow the Reverend Silas's advice spend the day in prayer and solemn reading of helpful, but rather gloomy, literature. The milder will allow a solemn game of chess on the Sabbath, as Sunday is invariably called by the evangelicals, but this is a relaxation frowned upon by those of sterner faith.

It is a revival of Puritanism in the Church of England, and with all its faults it is better than the mere coldness of the eighteenth century. Unfortunately, it has the worst vice of Puritanism, it attracts the oily hypocrite, the type that Dickens painted in his Mr Chadband and Mr Pecksniff. It is a hard, cold religion too, and attracts the hard, cold, commercial type of man, yet it does help many men and women to lead something of a decent life, and at least many of its professors are fiercely sincere; such men as Shaftesbury and many of his party belonged to this branch of the Church, and did credit to its teachings by their humanity.

Yesterday

We shall see a great change here in the course of the next fifty years, for already the preaching of Pusey and Newman and Keble are stirring the dry bones of the Church in Oxford. Soon will come earnest young men who fast on Fridays and during Lent have richly decorated altars, and who will abolish the three-decker and the box-pews, and intone the service. And after them yet others who try to bring the Church of England as near to its Mother Church, the ancient Catholic Church, as possible.

There was a new feature too in the industrial life of the town, the trade union. This was a society of workmen employed in any particular trade banded together to secure fair play for themselves as against the employers, and was certainly the natural result of the consistent attitude of the eighteenth-century employer. But in many ways it was an unfortunate result. True, by means of the strike, concerted refusal to work, which was now allowed to be lawful provided no violence was used, the employed could, in times of prosperity, secure an increased wage from their masters. But the organization had serious defects, some of which are by no means cured yet.

In the first place, the average workman could not realize that it is no use striking on a falling market, that a trade which is making little or no

233

profit cannot raise wages, however long the workmen remain out on strike. This led to many dis-
appointments, strikes that lingered for weeks and
months till the men were starved back to work at
the old or worse rates of wages. But disappointed
men will sometimes take to violence, and there
are always unscrupulous agitators who will urge
the men to violence in the hope of getting something for themselves out of the wreck.

Secondly, the trade union promoted from the
first the attitude that the interests of employer
and employed are diametrically opposite. But this
is certainly not the case, especially in an industrial
country that will not support its own population
except by the profits of that industry. In such a
country, and England is an example, if ill-con-
sidered action on either side damages trade the
workman, who has no reserve of wealth to tide
him over bad times, will be the first to suffer.
It is therefore not the wisest thing to set master
against man and create bad feeling by which the
trade that gives the workman his living will be
ruined.

Still, the men were not altogether to blame.
The masters as a whole were hostile not only to
the trade union, which was to be expected, but to
their aims, the securing of decent wages and conditions, which was foolish and short-sighted. They

might, in fact, have drawn the dragon's teeth by offering reasonable co-operation, as the best sort of employer was to do later, instead of which they allowed a spirit of bitterness to arise which still poisons relations between master and men.

There was another disquieting result of the trade union, and we can see it best by what happened in 1845 in Ellington. It was a time of trade depression, and at the same time things were dear and living very hard for the poor. The men, in view of high costs of living, demanded higher wages, the masters, in view of the loss they were suffering, demanded a reduction rather than an increase of wages. They consequently took a leaf from their men's book, and declared a lock-out, refusing to allow the men to work except on their own conditions.

The men's leaders denounced this as brutal tyranny, illogically enough, for if the lock-out is a brutal form of coercion, so is the strike, as both depend on the same principle, using the necessities of your opponent to force him to accept your point of view. But it was hard for them to see their wives and children starve, and the attempt to burn down the chief woollen mill in Ellington was the work of desperate men. The engineer "hoist with his own petard" found the experience unpleasant and broke out into furious rioting that took a great deal of putting down.

The English Town

However, a period of prosperity followed. For a new spirit of Imperialism was abroad, the old colonial Empire had become the United States of America, but the new Empire—Canada, Australia, India—was buying English goods as fast as English factories could make them. Conditions too were improving. Very slowly the central Government began to insist on local Governments doing their duty. The process was cautious, fearful of offending vested interests, but it went on all through the century. There were no spectacular schemes of reform, such as older Governments had indulged in to their ruin, but cautious nibbles here and there at the problem. And the first to be tackled was the scandal of Poor Law administration.

As has been explained, the greatest scandals here were caused by the use of public money to the benefit of the administrators of the Poor Law rather than of the poor. There was another difficulty too; in many parishes relief was granted by favour, and idle, able-bodied men were kept in their idleness at the cost of their harder working neighbours. The magistrates and overseers were supposed to provide work to do for the able-bodied pauper, but this would have meant the spending of time and money on providing and overseeing the work, so as often as not the importunate pauper was given food tickets on local shops (which,

of course, made a thumping profit on the business)
and left to idle.

Two things were done to prevent this. First a
system of unions was worked out, parishes were
grouped for Poor Law purposes instead of each
parish managing its own affairs, and in each union
was established a workhouse. Here the pauper
would be given food and lodging, but only on
condition of doing work. Outside relief, that is
money or food to persons not in the workhouse
was severely restricted. Thus it was hoped
to class the poor into three groups, those who
could not hope to make a living in the outer
world, and must therefore become inmates of the
workhouse, those who were in temporary distress
and might be relieved outside, and those who were
mere tramps and vagrants and should be punished
as such.

The workhouse system, though more successful
than the old uncontrolled local relief, was not as
great a success as its promoters hoped. They deliberately made the workhouse unpleasant to dis-
courage the work-shy. The result was to dis-
courage also the respectable poor who might have
needed its aid, most of whom would rather starve
or go to prison than to the " Union." Also it led
to trouble with the trade unions, who objected to
the competition of workhouse industries, which

were therefore confined to stone-breaking, oakum-picking, and other futile tasks resented by the workhouse inmates. The new system was also to save public money, a fact so well impressed on the administrators of it that they sometimes did so at the expense of the lives of those committed to their care, who starved slowly to death.

But of course the universal panacea was applied to the Poor Law as elsewhere. Guardians of the poor were to be elected for the future, and would in consequence be honest and impeccable. It is true that they did not suffer from quite the same temptations as their predecessors, but the system was by no means perfect. For when in early days the guardians were elected by a limited number of middle-class electors they were tempted to be stingy and harsh to keep down the rates, and when later on a larger electorate was given the duty of choosing these officials, the temptation was reversed. Toward the end of the nineteenth century and in the twentieth century we find party politics invading the sphere of Poor Law administration, and guardians recklessly spending public money, paying high rates of out-relief, and committing other abuses in order to gain the votes of those who profit by such misuse of power. Lately an Act has been passed transferring the duties of the guardians to County and Town Councils, which it is hoped will be less open to such influences.

Then in regard to industrial matters we find the same thing, the central Government interferes and insists, by means of factory acts, hours of work acts, and health laws, with the employers' control of his place of work. As in the case of the Poor Law the benefits of this advance have been partly nullified by the curse of party politics.

Look for a moment at a weaving mill in Ellington. In 1830 it is a dirty, gloomy shed, where workers toil for disgracefully long hours at disgracefully low wages, in insanitary conditions. The machinery is unguarded, and horrible accidents are common, also the death-rate from consumption is high. Gradually the hours of work are reduced by Government regulation, wages rise partly by a natural economic process, partly under pressure of strikes and threats of strikes. Gradually medical supervision, sanitary supervision, proper protection of machinery are enforced by Government inspectors, until to-day that mill is light and airy, clean and safe as machinery can ever be. To this nobody could take exception if only Government interference had stopped there.

Unfortunately there is another side to the picture. For the Tories who prophesied in 1832 that the franchise must be extended to everybody were right, and now almost every free, sane English man and woman has a vote at twenty-one years of age, which means that the working-class vote becomes the guiding factor in politics. But the working class, or their political leaders, demand far more than this. They insist on high rates and taxation, to be applied to bettering their own lot, a most natural desire, but one that has certain disadvantages in practice. For the employer cannot afford to employ at a loss and if a great deal of his profit is absorbed by the State he must of necessity cut down the number employed, or refrain from trying to expand his business, which means that he could not employ more people.

It is in the nineteenth century that we find in Ellington the first little group of workmen and others who are the nucleus of the modern Socialist party, so strong in the town to-day. These people have developed the theory that under the system of private ownership the workman's interests will never be given a fair field, and demand that the State should take over ownership of industry, for, they argue, the State would not be tempted to make profit by trade at the expense of the worker, and the worker would be more contented as a State servant for he, as a voter, is a part of the State, and would thus have a share of what profit was made.

Yesterday

It is impossible here to argue the pros and cons of Socialism. Suffice it to state that the theory took such a hold upon the working classes that to-day a Socialist member sits for the borough of Ellington in Parliament.

Such is the outline of town life during the last century. There are many other things that should be told, but are difficult, for the reasons explained at the beginning of the chapter, to deal with in this book. The final chapter will attempt to sketch very briefly the main tendencies of the present in English town life, and suggest where they may be leading.

CHAPTER XIX

To-day and To-morrow

ELLINGTON is a prosperous town now, containing some hundred thousand people, and very much changed indeed from the slow, solid town of the last century. The castle is no longer forlorn. It stands as a memorial of the town's past, and you may go over it on payment of a small fee, and, if you seem to know something about such things, the custodian, a learned man in his own way, will share with you little titbits of knowledge that he has acquired in the twenty years he has held that office.

Changed indeed is Castle Square. Gone are the florid Georgian, the prim Victorian houses. Shops and offices surround the grey pile of the castle, while motor-buses fuss and skirr around its base. The Square is the trade-centre of the town.

Staple Street, however, the gentlemen of King George III's reign would recognize even under King George V. It still consists of two rows of grey, serious houses, and it is here that the lawyers, doctors, and professional men of the town have their homes, old grey houses with old walled gardens, an oasis of peace in a busy city.

Down by the river slums have been cleared, and a broad walk set with gardens runs by the bank for the pleasure of the citizens on summer evenings. In other parts of the town the same thing is happening, and new housing estates are springing up outside in the suburbs for working men and women.

The old Grammar School has recently moved into new, wide buildings with fine playing fields, a gymnasium, and a modern laboratory. There are well-equipped secondary schools and numerous free primary schools in the town. The principle of free compulsory education has been accepted and is being extended.

The factories in the town are clean, well run, and the wages paid are sufficient if not the fabulous sums that the agitator has always held out as a bait to his dupes. The oldest firm in the place, Higgins, Sons and Company, founded by that rebel against eighteenth-century corruption of whom we have spoken, has playing-fields, a social club, a well-run bar, where good, clean liquor, not chemical poison, can be obtained, and an excellent pension scheme.

The municipal swimming-baths, run by the corporation, are excellent, so are the children's playgrounds, and the clinic for advising people as to their health and that of their children.

There is a fine hospital in the town that will hold not twelve but twelve hundred poor sick folk, and has paying wards for those not so poor who cannot afford nursing homes.

That is the bright side of the picture of to-day. Now to look at the dark. In the main it can be put into one short sentence. Democracy, government of the people for the people by the people, may be an excellent thing—at any rate, many great men have held it to be so—but it is undeniably very expensive. The taxation, both central and local, that the men of Ellington have to pay to-day is very heavy indeed. Anything like that taxation, allowing for differences in wealth, would have raised a rebellion under the most powerful of medieval tyrants. But in the end it is the ordinary working man who pays taxation, and grumble as you will it cannot be avoided. The rich man will pay his fair share, but attempts to tax the rich specially merely react on the poor. For the average rich man's wealth is not in ready money: a large amount of it is locked up in productive enterprise. For taxes, however, he must raise ready cash, and if he has to withdraw his wealth from industry to pay taxation then industry must either reduce wages or employment.

To-day and To-morrow

In this century, owing to the trade union attitude on wages, the other alternative is inevitable, so that we can divide the workers into two categories, the aristocrats of labour, enjoying high wages and good conditions, the residue in an almost permanent condition of unemployment because industry cannot both employ them and pay the rates and taxes demanded.

The fault lies exactly where it has lain all through English history, the central Government is largely to blame. The services now provided by the State make a striking contrast to the *laissez-faire* Governments of the eighteenth and nineteenth centuries, who left the workman to settle his own problems. So too does the State interference between master and man. For instance, when there was a coal strike in Ellington a little while ago Government officials attempted to patch up the quarrel.

But the central Government depends for its support in the Commons on votes, and there is a suspicion among all classes that in consequence the interference of the Government may be biased. Should there be a Conservative Government in office, the workers fear that their decision will be biased by the fact that most employers are their supporters; in the case of interference by a Labour Government the employers fear that the Government is more anxious to conciliate their supporters than to do justice. This keeps the town in a constant state of unrest, class against class, interest against interest, and lowers the already low condition of trade, thus increasing unemployment.

There is also the suspicion that Governments will introduce measures affecting the very life and security of the town from party motives rather than national. This or that costly scheme of educational or social reform, whose benefits are problematical and, if real, certainly distant, is introduced apparently to make sure of the support of some clamorous group that advocates it rather than for any more solid reason, at a time when fresh taxation is an evil to be deplored.

Lastly—and of this vice government must be cured, or some other form of government will replace democracy—these things, costly in themselves, are made infinitely more costly by the methods of administration. Especially is this true of local government. It is an open secret that the Ellington Corporation could do with far fewer employees, but of course any party who proposed such a thing would lose votes at the next election, so that nothing at all is done. Also there has been a scandal about some Corporation housing estates. Men with influence, friends of members of the Corporation, have obtained contracts in connexion with the work, and the work was badly done. The matter was hushed up, but it leaves a nasty taste in the mouth.

Above all there is a feeling throughout the town of insecurity. Successive Governments seem to raise taxation, not by the most useful and economical means, but by the means that will do least damage to their own supporters, most damage to those whose votes are unimportant. Now, as we have seen, absolute indifference on the part of the State to trade and commercial relations between man and man is bad, but it is questionable whether biased interference is not worse. The State has taken on the task of acting as umpire between employer and employed and seeing that neither side takes unfair advantage of the other. If it does so, well and good. But what if the State surreptitiously aids one side or the other, weighting the scales of justice in favour of the party that will be most likely to support the existing Government? Then in the end State interference will be worse than no interference at all, and will lead to a demand for no interference.

The old standards are toppling too, and no man seems to know what the morrow will bring forth. Aeroplanes hover and boom over the town. Is England still safe from invasion? One man says yes, one says no; neither can be proved right. The War has left its mark. The burning question

The English Town

which divides the town is, not whether peace is desirable, but whether we are going the right way to obtain it. Colonel Hawkes, the Territorial Commanding Officer, will tell you one thing, Councillor Dill who would like to abolish the Territorials, will tell you another, and whom are you to believe?

Free trade! Twenty years ago to have questioned the wisdom of free imports into England would have led to the questioner being laughed out of Ellington, for Ellington throve on cheap food, and there was little foreign competition in those goods that the town manufactured. To-day there is a strong party in the town that believes that Free Trade is a worn-out policy, and should be replaced by something else.

That is the dark side of life in Ellington to-day in secular affairs. Let us take a last look at the church. Certainly Parson Akers or the Reverend Silas Connington would not recognize it, but clergymen of an older date might well think themselves back in their own familiar church. Gone is the whitewash; the noble carved stone of the church shows clear and unstained. Gone is the clumsy three-decker. A neat pulpit at one side of the church, reading-desks in the choir, leave unencumbered the worshipper's view of a fine stone altar that a clergyman of Ellington discovered some years ago buried away in a disused cellar.

To-day and To-morrow

There is a little side-chapel decked with flags to the memory of the men who died between 1914 and 1918, and many a mother and wife comes there to pray for her dead loved ones. Holy Communion—the present vicar calls it " Mass "—is celebrated every day, not three times a year as formerly.

One may like or dislike the change, but certainly religion is alive. The difficulty is that the congregations are small, for many men dislike the dogma of this new revival, and others are careless. Will religion in the end win, and bring back to the Church her lost members? No one can say.

The other churches in the town are in the same difficulty. Even one clergyman of a certain small group, who has taken to allowing smoking in his church and offering cinematograph entertainments, cannot fill his church.

In the matter of amusements for the ordinary people there has been improvement in one way and retrogression in another. We have the cinematograph, football teams, greyhound races, dirt-track races, and golf. But there is something of the Roman gladiator show about too many of them. Unfortunately in too many cases a few paid men perform the exercise and run the risk, the rest look on and bet, unlike that older Merrie England where a man was expected to take a man's part in sport. Still, for those that will, there are opportunities for personal exercise, and they are increasing.

Perhaps, of all the inventions that have revolutionized town life in England the motor-car is the most conspicuous. For the motor-car and motor-omnibus enable men to live at some distance from their work, and the main cause of industrial over-crowding, desire to be near the worker's place of employment, is no longer so urgent. Also the town worker can now for little cost get a day or so in the country to refresh his energies, an excellent thing if and when he is taught to respect the country, not to litter it with tin cans. But perhaps that will come.

Lastly, what of to-morrow? Clearly the main tendency of to-day is twofold. In the first place the machine increasingly takes the place of human effort. In a way this is a good thing if it relieves the monotonous drudgery of certain unskilled work. But it will be a very bad thing if the machine is allowed to rule the man, if art, poetry, love of life, and beauty are forgotten in the desire for more and more perfect machines, as they were in the eighteenth century in the desire for more and more money.

The second great tendency of the day is this, that each year Government tends to take more and more responsibility for the governed. Again there is no harm in this in moderation, but already there are signs that moderation is being over-passed. That the worker should be protected from deliberate oppression is right, that he should be shepherded from cradle to grave till he cannot call his soul or body his own is wrong and foolish. That the boy who wants and can use an education should be given it if he cannot pay is right and just. The proposition that education must be forced on to those who do not want and cannot use it is at least much more doubtful.

Above all, where the Government interferes it must interfere impartially, otherwise interference is worse than useless, and can lead only to bad feeling between class and class and consequent inefficiency. I am not prepared to prophesy whether our present system of Government can shake itself sufficiently free of class and party interest to become a just and impartial arbiter in industrial affairs. I am prepared to prophesy that if it does not it will go, and some other system will take its place that can do so.

I have tried to the best of my ability to sketch the growth of an English town from the forest village to a modern industrial community. That in such an enterprise in the space of a small book many things have been omitted that ought to have been treated is inevitable. That my own political opinions are not concealed I am aware, but it is impossible to write a book like this from a neutral point of view; I can only say that I have tried to be as fair as possible to people whom I do not like. Finally, I shall consider my work well rewarded if this book should stimulate any reader to inquire for himself into the fascinating history of England, not the dry dates and names that are its background, but the vivid, eager life of our country in the past, whence we draw the familiar things of our own every day.

INDEX

The English Town

Index

Moral effects of the Renaissance, 145–146
Motor transport, 250
Mystery and Morality plays, 134–135

Napoleonic wars, the effects of, 221
Norman Conquest, the, effects of, on English life, 52–53

Parliament, Simon de Montfort's, 81 ; of 1295, 88 ; grievances brought before, 88 ; methods of election to, in the fifteenth century, 122–123 ; deals with vagrants, 156 ; opposition of, to the Stuarts, 172–173 ; Royalist character of, at the Restoration, 178 ; position of, in the eighteenth century, 203 ; 'rotten' and 'pocket' boroughs represented in, 205 ; reform of, 225
Pauperism, development of, in the late Middle Ages, 128 ; in the eighteenth century, 207–208. *See also* Poor Law *and* Towns
Peasants' Revolt, the, causes of, 107–111 ; suppression of, 113–114
Pie Powder, the Court of, 96
Pilgrimage of Grace, the, 152–153
Pilgrims, 45
Piracy, 99, 124
Poll-tax, 110 ; fraudulent evasion of, 111 ; attack on collectors of, 112
Poor Law, first, 156 ; Elizabethan, 157 ; abuses of, in the eighteenth century, 206–208 ; reforms of, 236–238
Popish Plot, the, 183–185
Punishments, 83, 129, 202
Puritanism, doctrines of, 158 ; danger of hypocrisy in, 158–159 ; influence of, in towns, 167, 168 ; feud between Presbyterians and Independents, 174 ; triumph of, 175–177 ;

attack on, by the Restoration Government, 179

Radical party, programme of, 219 ; attitude of, toward the Factory Acts, 230–231
Railways, 229–230
Reform Bill, the, reasons for, 221–225 ; nature of, 226
Reformation, the, causes of, 150 ; by whom approved, 150, 152 ; character of, 164
Regulation of wages and prices, 120
Renaissance, the, 139–142
Roman Catholic Church, the, attitude of, to commerce and morals, 150–151 ; affection of poorer classes for, 151–152 ; position of, under Charles II, 183–184 ; policy of James II toward, 186 ; in the eighteenth century, 199
Roman times, village life in, 13–17 ; towns in, 18

Saxons, the, coming of, 19–23 ; ships of, 21
Schools, beginnings of, 82 ; methods of teaching in, 83–84 ; value of, in English life, 84
Sheep-farming, 107–108
Signs, over shops, etc., 75
Social conditions, in the Middle Ages, 132 ; in the sixteenth century, 163–167 ; in the eighteenth century, 205–207
Spain, war with, the popularity of, with merchants, 170 ; failure of the war with, under Cromwell, 176–177
Star Chamber, the, economic work of, 166–167 ; abolition of, 172
Stuarts, the, English policy under, 170–171 ; unpopularity of, in the towns, 171, 172

Tories, the, 183–184, 195, 198 ; attitude of, to the Industrial Revolution, 219 ; change in attitude of, 220 ; and the Re-

255